Touching His Cloak

A Journey to Healing

Tammy Stanek, RN

ISBN 978-1-7333199-7-3

This book is dedicated to

Jesus, my Savior and best friend

Michele, my daughter, confidant, soulmate, and spiritual helper

Timothy and Andrew, my sons, for their strength, love, and constant encouragement

Barbara Berger, my spiritual mom and spiritual director

With special thanks to
Elizabeth Morath for the title and cover ideas

.

Table of Contents

Introduction

Affliction brings out graces that cannot be seen in a time of health. It is the treading of the grapes that brings out the sweet juices of the vine; so it is affliction that draws forth submission, weans us from the world, and invites complete rest in God. Use afflictions while you have them.
-Robert Murray McCheyn

How often have we thought, "I have faith, so why am I not healed?" My hope and prayer is that, through these pages, you will journey with me to find the answer. Before I share my story and research, I offer a statement for contemplation: God is pure love. He is passionately in love with each one of us.

Let that penetrate. *God is passionately in love with you!* This foundational belief is intricately woven into the tapestry of healing. When we enter fully into this love relationship, miracles happen!

God tells us, "'For I know the plans that I have for you,' declares the Lord, 'plans for welfare and not for calamity to give you a future and a hope. Then you will call upon Me and come and pray to Me, and I will listen to you. You will seek Me and find Me when you search for Me with all your heart. I will be found by you,' declares the Lord" (Jer. 29: 11–14 [NASB]).

I am excited for you because I know the wonderful things God has in store for you. When you come to know God—not know *of* Him or know *about* Him, but truly come to know *Him* as a person—your life will change. And when you come to truly know who you *are* in Him, the floodgates will open.

I would like to mention that this book was intended for everyone, regardless of religious affiliation. I share insights from both Catholic and Protestant sources, as well as from secular and medical authorities. At the height of my suffering, I did not put much stock in the helpful suggestions from those around me because they had no idea what I was going through. They did not understand my suffering! I have decided to write this book because I do understand; I have lived it. Because of it, I have come to believe that God will do the most loving thing in the most loving way for the greatest amount of good.

The title of this book is a reference to the story found in Luke 8: 43–48 about a woman who reached out to touch Jesus's cloak and was healed. I connect with this woman on many levels; I, too, have suffered with a cruel affliction that took my health, my finances, my job, my home, and my life as I knew it. However, the woman in that story beckons us to imitate her in her faith and ability to trust in the goodness of the only One who could save her. This book reflects a modern account of this story and will hopefully help you to trust in His good-ness so that you, too, may reach to touch Him with anticipation and wonder-filled expectancy.

I am my beloved's and His desire is for me . . . Come, let us go.
(Song of Sol. 7:1)

CHAPTER 1

My Story

You can never learn that Christ is all you need,
until Christ is all you have.
-Corrie Ten Boom

My doctor said I would never be able to make the four-hour drive to Ohio for the Franciscan University of Steubenville, Ohio's annual Catholic Charismatic Conference. At this point in my healing journey, I was still ambulatory but unable to sit for more than two to three minutes. The pain I suffered on a daily basis was excruciating. I could not sit. I could not stand still. I could not bend or take care of myself. My days were spent mostly alone, lying in bed. I so desperately wanted to go to this conference, believing in God's love for me and that I would be healed. My daughter drove me while I lay in the back of a van with my back packed in ice. I had such a positive spirit and was so in love with Jesus. I just knew He was going to help me.

During the "miracle service," I was ready to receive! I had expectant faith and eagerly watched as they brought Jesus in the Blessed

Sacrament. The lights were dimmed; the smell of incense wafted through the air of the fieldhouse. My heart pounded as the procession with the Blessed Sacrament came up the aisle. The song "Agnus Dei" by Michael W. Smith played in the background. People praised God as the spotlight shone on the large Host in the monstrance. *Jesus was coming!* A deacon from our hometown stood up, shouting, "I am healed! My shoulder is healed!" Over two hundred people received healing that evening.

My hope grew as the Blessed Sacrament came close. I felt as if Jesus was standing right there in front of me, His beautiful eyes looking into my soul and tenderly smiling . . . but then He walked away. I was devastated. *Why, Jesus, did you pass me by?*

I suddenly had an image of my mother. Unsure of exactly what it meant, I became aware at that moment that I still harbored very bad feelings toward her. I began to pray for her and forgave her, even though I thought I had forgiven her in the past. Just then, I felt deep in my heart that Jesus was saying, "I am going to ease your pain, but you will not receive your healing tonight. Do not be disappointed. I have not forgotten you! I would like you to receive healing from a priest in your diocese."

This moment was a turning point in my quest for wellness. Growing up Protestant, I was very familiar with "faith healing" and believed fully in God working through the gifts and charisms of the Holy Spirit. However, this pivotal encounter would eventually lead me on a path of learning about the ministry of healing and, more importantly, about my relationship with God in a way I had not known was possible. That night, I believed that Jesus was going to help me. He did but not in the way I expected or wanted at the time. As I reflect on that evening, God gave me so much more than I realized. The blessings of that moment far outweighed the temporary feeling of disappointment. Although I did not understand at the time, He did not pass me by. He did not disappoint!

The Early Years

In February of 1963, my mom gave birth to me and almost died of pneumonia. I was raised for the first many days of my life by multiple nurses in a downtown Buffalo, New York Catholic hospital. Fearing I would not be able to survive the virus that was already taking over my little body, the nurses did not allow me to bond with my mom. Later in life, she told me that I, preferring the care of the nurses, seemed distant toward her when we were finally allowed be together. Although she did not realize it at the time, these early moments wounded her. It is amazing how little events in life can leave hidden scars buried deep within our psyche.

That same year, I was asleep at home in my crib in my parents' room while my mom ran next door to get something. In that brief time, my three-year-old brother found a pack of matches. Striking it like he saw his daddy do, he caused a flame to erupt from the tiny tip, scaring him and causing him to drop it—on my parents' bed. He ran and hid as it burst into flame. By the grace of God, my grandpa, who was on his morning stroll, saw flames and smoke coming from the bedroom window where I was fast asleep. He grabbed me and my brother and pulled us to safety. God saved me that day.

A couple of years later, I was a toddler, and my brother was just entering school. We lived next door to my aunt and uncle and were frequently "watched" by my uncle, who apparently was a known alcoholic and "toucher"—the dark family secret. From my earliest memories, sexual touching was a constant and a frightening source of a developing insecurity. I remember trying to never be alone with him and always trying to know where he was in the house.

Then one day, when I was around eight, I went into the basement of my aunt and uncle's house. I had no idea he was home, much less sitting down there in the darkness. I felt a hand come from behind me and grab me. I could smell the alcohol on his breath; he warned me not to make a sound. With his body pressed against mine from behind, he guided me into his workshop.

I was in shock. I don't think I could have screamed if I wanted to. For years, I blamed myself for getting raped. *Why didn't I scream? Why didn't I run?* After he had had his satisfaction, I remember staggering upstairs and out into the snow, wandering down the street looking for my aunt.

I was paralyzed. I couldn't talk, couldn't cry. When she found me, my aunt yelled at me for not wearing a coat and guided me back to the house. I felt betrayed by my family. They *knew* he was a molester, yet they continued to leave me alone with him. That day, as the numbness turned into fear, I vowed to start taking care of myself. When I finally got up the courage to tell my mom and aunt what he had done, their response was, "What do you want us to do? Put him in jail? You should know better to stay away from him!" The anger welled deep: The people who were supposed to protect me *blamed* me.

I remember what I was wearing that day. I had put on a dress and felt like a little lady, but in that moment, my little girl childhood was ripped away. I never wanted to be in "girl clothes" again. *Where was God in this? Why didn't He protect me? Why did He allow this?* I began to think differently about God that day.

Later that year, in spring 1971, I went to school as I did every day with my Partridge Family lunchbox in hand and sat in the back. That particular morning, our teacher decided to do a visual experiment to demonstrate the five senses. All was well until he highlighted the sense of sight. I was a bit nervous as he reached for a can of gasoline, poured it in a pie tin, and pulled out match. With that fateful strike, a great explosion ensued, and my teacher was completely engulfed in flames. I remember hearing, "Run, children, run!" as he ran past us to the damp earth of the front lawn to extinguish the flames. I remember the singed hair on the children in the front row and the screams of terror as we watched our teacher burn alive. The smell of gas and smoke hung heavy in the air.

The school put us on buses to send us home. As I walked the half-mile down the street to my house, I was in shock. I reached my drive-way and walked up the front stoop. The door was locked, and I rang the doorbell. When my mother opened the door, I was shaking, tears carving a path down my sooty cheeks.

I just stood there. She kept asking what happened, but I couldn't talk. She grabbed me frantically, shaking me until I spoke. I screamed hysterically, "My teacher was on fire!"

Then, it happened again—the typical reaction from my mother: "Why didn't you save him? Why didn't you throw a coat over him?"

Defeated by my mother's response, I took the weight of responsibility for something I had no control over. He was a big man and I was a small child, yet most of my life I blamed myself. While the trauma itself left deep scars, the belief that I had no one to take care of me ran deeper. There were nights when I would wake in terror, running to my mom's room, only to be told I needed a psychiatrist. I probably did need help, but the spirit of how she said it told me she thought I was weak—"sick in the head," as she often retorted. No hugs. No consolation. No hope.

By the time I was ten, I wanted to die. I used to pray for God to take me. In a time before media-sensationalized suicide, I did not even know killing oneself was possible, so I prayed for God to take me. My mom did take me to Jesus John Alvarez, a monk from Spain who prayed over me. The spirit of suicide left me, at least for a while. By God's grace, I had the will to go on living. A little voice inside me would say, "You have things to do!" and gave me hope that someday things might change.

If you are wondering where my dad was in all of this, he was either at work (second shift) or in the hospital. He had MS and was a very sickly man. I never really knew him.

These are just a few examples of the physical and emotional abuse that daily marked my childhood. With each passing day, I survived by becoming hard inside; I figured if no one could love me and take care of me, I would take care of myself. I wanted someone to love me, but all I received at home was distance and abuse. I felt myself growing stronger emotionally as the anger burrowed deeper in my soul.

The Marriage

Fast forward a couple of years to 1976. I was admitted to a local prep school on a full academic scholarship, a very brief reprieve in my very painful life. At that point, I had chosen to walk away from my faith, hoping the world would give me the happiness and love I so desperately sought. As the years passed, however, the loneliness and rage increased. I was able to keep these feelings hidden for a while. Then, my dad's illness progressed, and home life became intolerable. The suicidal thoughts returned.

I distinctly remember April 15, 1980 when I realized I could not go on like I was anymore. I prayed to God for a change. I cried out for help. It was also that night that I met my future husband.

My, how one decision changed the trajectory of my life! I was on a date, roller-skating with the nice young man whose father owned the rink. My date left the rink for a bit, but I stayed on the skate floor, got distracted, and fell. My future husband literally swept me off my feet. He picked me up, and his charm had me hooked in minutes. He looked like Robert Redford and was just as magnetizing.

I often wonder what would have happened if I had remained with the young man I came with. God gives us a "sixth sense," a little voice, a guardian angel. I knew something was not right but was far too young, naïve, and wounded to understand.

There were glaring signs that he was an abuser. Perhaps I chose not to see because I was desperately seeking an escape from my home. Before we got married, I suggested we take a break; he threatened to kill himself, blaming me for not loving him. I did marry him in October 1981 and remember that as I was preparing to walk down the aisle, instead of feeling joy, darkness enveloped me. I truly believed if I just loved him, he would change. Unfortunately, love does not work that way.

The signs of abuse were subtle at first, but by the end of the marriage, when he saw he was losing control over me, he grew more dangerous. Throughout my marriage, I became an expert at keeping the peace, so much so that when I finally left, people were shocked to learn that anything was wrong in the relationship. I am thankful that, for a while, I was able to keep my kids somewhat sheltered and safe so that they could enjoy some normal moments of childhood. But I could not shelter them forever. When my husband began to use violence to keep control, my children began to see the truth. I will never forget that my daughter, who was eleven years old at the time, was so happy when I told her that I was going with them to a new home. While I was trying to stay with my abusive husband "for the sake of the children," they were relieved at the thought of finally not having to live in fear. How destructive was the advice I was given to "just try harder."

I will share a few examples of what came to be part of daily life.

My husband used to check the odometer before I went to church or the grocery store, just to make sure I was going where I said. No stopping at a friend's for a cup of coffee. No stopping at the park to let the kids play. No freedom to make any move unless he allowed it. Humiliating me in public was another favorite activity of his, as well as giving me the "look" to make sure I "behaved." The unpredictability of his outbursts made every movement a mine field. And, as a result of my abusive childhood, I thought this treatment was okay!

Over time, my eyes began to open to the truth—both of him and the state of our marriage. Soon after we were wed, I was pregnant. He took me to the Adirondack Mountains two weeks before I was due. We sat in a canoe at dusk in the middle of a small lake. With one poorly calculated move, the canoe capsized. The water was cold and dark. As I flailed frantically, he said, "I am ready to die now. How 'bout you?" That moment shook me to my core: Not only had my husband put me in a very dangerous place, but he was doing nothing to help his wife and unborn child! I thought, "He may want to give up, but I refuse!"

I started screaming for help for what seemed like an hour. The sky darkened, and the fight-or-flight instinct kicked in. I prayed God would save me as I struggled for a shore that I could not even see. I had been distant from God, even though I had been going through prayer motions. This prayer was different. I knew He was there and would help me; I was going to keep screaming and praying until I was saved. I guess my faith was still there; I heard the faint voice of an older man. He told me he was coming to help. After a short while, he and his wife came in a paddleboat and dragged us to shore. I was so pregnant and weak that I could not get into the boat, so I just held onto the back while they headed for shore. Instead of helping me, my husband got in the boat, reinforcing what I already knew: I could depend on no one and had to take care of myself. Funny how I could think that after God had just saved me.

Two weeks later, my daughter was born. She was precious, and I immediately fell in love. For first time, I experienced the miracle of a new life, and the joy was unlike anything I had ever known. Not so for my husband. Three days after her birth, I knew something was wrong. My baby girl started hiccupping in her bassinet; he stood over her, screaming obscenities and telling her to die.

He was becoming more terrifying by the day. While we had re-prieves when he worked long hours and went on week-long business trips, abuse was part of daily life. Because I was so skilled at defusing tensions and placating him, no one knew the terror I was living. We went to church, the beach, and amusement parks as a family. Everyone thought he was such a great guy, that everything was normal.

About ten years into the marriage, when my son was about six, my husband falsely accused me of having an affair. He took my son, stripped him naked, threw him in the side yard, and started beating him and kicking him like an animal. My innocent little boy screamed, "Mommy, save me!" My husband said if I came one step closer, it would be worse for both of us. My heart was in agony as I helplessly watched my child being abused. As he was beating my son, he shouted at me, "This is your fault! If you would stay in line, I wouldn't have to do this!" I was frozen, trying to figure out how to best save us. Somehow, I managed to lure him away from my son. Later, I blamed myself: How could any mother not throw herself in the path of danger to protect her child? But I thought, *If he kills me, I won't be able to help my kids.*

When I did share the difficulties of my marriage, I was met with unhelpful advice: I had made my bed, so now I must lie in it. Even our trusted Episcopal priest friend told me I must stay with him because I made an oath before God. But a year later, my husband in a drunken rage tried to kill our pets in front of the children. I was able to keep the children hidden from him for a bit and then, by the grace of God, re-membered I was supposed to be at a local church to play keyboard for Mass. He had been out of work for almost a year, and we desperately needed the money. I put the kids in the car and waited for him to jot down the mileage. The smell of alcohol wafted in the car as he made his last threat. Panicked and praying for God to guide me, I then drove to the Episcopal priest's house instead of to church.

I stood on the doorstep with the same numbness I had felt as a child—tears streaming down my cheeks, unable to talk. The children and I stayed there for a few days while he tried to talk to my husband. When the priest returned, he told me to go back to my husband, that my husband loved me and had promised to go to counseling. Although I knew my husband was lying to regain control over me, I fought my instincts and returned.

Sensing the growing danger, I desperately prayed once again for God's help. God helped me in the past, so He just had to help me now! During one of those nights that I lay in the dark, next to a man that I greatly feared, I remember praying the Chaplet of Divine Mercy. Though I was not yet Catholic, I had recently learned this very special prayer. From that moment, God seemed to begin to free me from my prison, putting people and support that I would soon need in my path. Things were eerily quiet for a year, but soon the episodes began again and intensified.

One of the people God placed in my path was a Catholic priest who essentially saved my life. Fr. Gil Weil was the priest at the county church where I was playing music for Mass. Under his guidance and teaching, I became Catholic during that tumultuous year.

One afternoon, while the kids were at school, I went to the rectory for catechesis. The opportunity presented itself: I burst into tears and told him everything. I had kept the secret for so long that I felt a weight lift off of me, if even for a moment. With his big blue eyes so full of compassion, he looked at me and said, "My God, woman! Get out! God loves you! He does not want you to be abused!"

My world was shaken. *Leave? But how?* Everyone had been telling me to stay because I made a commitment . . . and this advice from a Catholic priest? For weeks, I was in shock. I did not know what to do, but God showed me. As I had been praying and discerning the Catholic faith, I went to a little adoration chapel in the neighboring town. There, God spoke to my heart and helped me see.

I never intended to become Catholic; the faith seemed to be yet another weapon my "Catholic" husband used against me. He would make us say a rosary as a family, but if one of the children misspoke a word, the rage and violence ensued. Yet God was clearly calling me into the Catholic Church. After studying and praying for years, I knew I could not deny it any longer: Jesus was truly present in the Eucharist. God wanted me to be here, and I could not be anywhere else.

Once I made the decision to leave him, every help I needed suddenly appeared. God was making a way! For that next few months, even as the escape plan was set in motion, I endured so much—even rape. (Yes, rape is rape, even if the attacker is your husband.) Though I felt dirty and sick inside, I could endure anything because God was going to help me.

Those months seemed like eternity. I hardly slept, sleeping only when he was drunkenly passed out, afraid he would kill me in my sleep. But I had hope! Freedom was out there for me and my children, and I just needed to hang on until all the pieces were in place. Fearing my husband, I suffered in silence; my family, my friends, and even my children were unaware. I did not want anyone else to be exposed to possible harm.

If it were not for God's Divine Assistance, I would not be alive today. My body and my spirit endured twelve years of stress and abuse, and these are just a few of the examples of the trauma I experienced. These moments, however, were integral in moving me from a place of anger and mistrust—even in my relationship with God—to a place of distorted self-sufficiency, a place where no one would ever control me again. These events shaped the next period of my life, which would break me.

Before we go any further, if you or anyone you know is concerned about an abusive relationship, here are some questions to ask. Does anyone in your life:

- criticize you, humiliate you, or put you down?
- treat you so badly that you're embarrassed for your friends or family to see?
- ignore or put down your opinions or accomplishments?
- blame you for their own abusive behavior?
- see you as property or a sex object, rather than as a person?
- have a bad and unpredictable temper?
- hurt you, or threaten to hurt or kill you?
- threaten to take your children away or harm them?
- threaten to commit suicide if you leave?
- force you to have sex?
- destroy your belongings?
- act excessively jealous and possessive?
- control where you go or what you do?

- keep you from seeing your friends or family?
- limit your access to money, the phone, or the car?
- constantly check up on you?[1]

If you are answering yes or are even unsure, please seek help and guidance now!

Breaking and Freedom

In the late winter of 1995, I was finally able to move out, bringing my first taste of freedom. I was so stressed that day, having been awake all night and also having moved heavy furniture to prepare. I kept my mood light for the children's sake. When the final piece of furniture was placed in a little apartment across town, I stood in my daughter's new room and cried. Tears flowed until no tears were left; I cried so hard my stomach hurt.

I had never lived on my own and had three young children to care for. I did not even know how to write a check because my husband had kept me so isolated. I think people often stay in these situations because the fear of the unknown can be crippling; those demons of our imagination can be far worse than reality.

We were on welfare for a year while I looked for a job. I worked and went to nursing school, but my health was deteriorating. Stopping or resting was not an option, so I pressed on. The kids grew rebellious; my ex-husband sabotaged everything I tried to do. He gave me no support, both financially or with the children. As they grew, so did the problems. I was diagnosed with fibromyalgia and degenerative disc disease, making the already heavy burden more difficult to bear.

In 2003, I came home from a new job and found my teenaged son barely conscious from alcohol poisoning. As I sat on the floor, talking with poison control and weeping, I rocked him. I cried, "God, I can't handle this weight anymore! I can't do this!"

Two very broken lives sat on that bedroom floor amid the tears and vomit until my son became conscious again. All I could picture was Mary holding Jesus after He was taken down from the cross. I rocked my son, kissing his head and praying he would be okay. I asked Mary to help my kids because I was not doing a very good job raising them. I cried myself to sleep that night, knowing I could not go on like that anymore. Though God had heard my prayer and was rescuing me, I could not see it at the time; all I saw was God letting me down like everyone in my life had.

The next day, I bent to pick up a fork off the floor, and a lightning bolt seared through my body. My back finally gave out. Within the next year, I lost the house I had worked so hard to provide for my kids. I had worked nights, so I could go to school while they were at school, and I had sacrificed to give my kids some stability. In an instant, I lost my health and my freedom.

A self-sufficient person, I never wanted any help from anyone. Not being able to put on my own socks or wash my body was humiliating. I felt stripped of my dignity. I lost my friends. Life went on, and they continued without me. Though I do not blame them—they had to do what was best for their own lives—many moments left me feeling forgotten or replaced.

Visits from people became rare. I lost my job, which was once a source of pride and self-sufficiency. I could no longer participate in music ministry. My daughter was at college; my teenaged sons were both addicted and living either with their dad or at school. I was alone. I was scared. I was angry. *If God loves me, why isn't He helping me? How could He let this happen if He loves me?*

The anger turned to rage. All the hurts, disappointments, and pain I had endured became a reason to blame God. I unleashed on Him all that was buried deep within me. As I lay alone in my bed one afternoon, I let God have it. When the last bit of venom was out, the tears began. As the evening sun was fading, a warm ray of light rested upon the crucifix hanging in my room, illuminating Jesus's crucified body.

What had I just done? I had unleashed all my pain on Him, who had taken all *from* me and *for* me. I apologized and wept, but in that moment of sorrow and remorse, the strangest thing happened: As I looked at His body, I felt a love like I had never known. A deep peace filled the room. I was not alone. I felt Jesus there with me.

Slowly, as if a dense fog was dissipating, I was beginning to see the truth. With each thing taken from me, a veil was being lifted. I thought my happiness was dependent upon my independence, my job, my kids, my friends; with each loss, I began to see more clearly. I began to finally see Jesus. One thing and then another, gone. One veil and then another lifted. *He* was what I needed!

After my initial diagnosis, life was very challenging. I had no money. I could not take care of myself. I had no food. But somehow, a meal would show up. An unexpected check would come in the mail. A parishioner would stop by to see if I needed anything. I slowly realized that God was providing for every need. I could do nothing except trust Him, and the more I let Him, the more He did. What should have been a depressing, anxiety-filled time turned out to be the beginning of a healing I desperately needed. I was seeing that I did not need to carry the weight by myself.

The one my heart had searched for, the one I could depend on, the one I could finally trust was there all along. I just could not see Him through the blinding storm of anger and pain. For the first time in many years, I felt the anticipation of a child. As soon as I began to let go of those destructive feelings, God began filling me with the clarity, peace, and security I desired.

During the next few years, I had the first of two back surgeries that, I would learn, actually made my issues worse. I sought every treatment available with no results. I was not finding any relief through medicine, so I began to seek out healing from God through prayer groups, healing services, and learning everything I could about spiritual healing. I read Kenneth Hagin, Francis MacNutt, Charles Capp, books on the saints and spiritual warfare. I listened to talks by Katie Sousa and others. It was a slow, painful time filled with many disappointments and unanswered questions. *Why didn't God heal me yet? Was I doing something wrong?*

When I went to that conference in Steubenville and heard healing minister Damian Stayne, those words that I thought were from Jesus filled my brain: "I am going to ease your pain, but you will not receive your healing tonight. Do not be disappointed. I have not forgotten you. I would like you to receive healing from a priest in your diocese."

What was I missing? As I pondered the events of the conference, I remembered how I had thought of my mother. I had no idea the depth of those wounds until I sought counsel from a spiritual director and a very wise priest. He anointed me after I had gone to confession. I could feel something happening deep within me but not the physical healing I yearned for.

As a Protestant, I used to think Catholics were crazy for telling others their sins, but Reconciliation eventually became a special haven of grace. Every time I would go, the priest would help me see patterns of sin and areas of unforgiveness that I could not see for myself. And the grace! I can't describe it well, but something powerful would happen with each encounter. I could feel something changing inside. I was becoming less angry. I was living the forgiveness that I voiced.

I was given the grace to make amends with my mother and with my husband. He had been abusive to me until he took his last breath. The day he died, my sister-in-law found him collapsed. I rushed over, and she allowed me some privacy before the coroner came. He had bled out from esophageal varices, a common way for alcoholics to succumb. As I stood over him, I thought to myself, "So this is how it ends! You die in a puddle of your own blood."

So many emotions surged through me—anger, sadness, regret, blame. I am sure he caused many of my physical problems, and I felt robbed and cheated out of the beautiful experiences I should have had as a wife and mother. But he could not hurt me anymore. It was over. Relieved, I took a deep breath and prayed. Part of me wanted justice, for him to suffer as he made us suffer; yet I did not want it to end like that, knowing I could never take this moment back. I asked Jesus to be with him and be merciful to him, and I asked Jesus to help me.

As I prayed, the Holy Spirit gave me sight. If I did not forgive, then his destructive power would continue. The wounds would fester; healing would never come. I knelt near his lifeless body and voiced my forgiveness for all the horrible things he had done. I let go, even though I did not feel different. I let go, even though I could not reclaim what I had lost. I left knowing I did the right thing, even if he did not deserve mercy.

Due to my illnesses, I struggled to live a normal life. I used what little strength I had to go to doctors, church, spiritual direction, or errands only when absolutely necessary. The pain was so consuming, and due to an allergy to pain medication, I found little relief. Sometimes, the pain became so severe that I would go into shock and be rushed to the hospital, only to be told there was nothing they could do.

During my convalescence, I had gone to twelve doctors, none of whom could diagnose the problem. I was told I was crazy and actually thrown out of one highly respected doctor's office because he said I was a liar. I was so vulnerable and scared only to be abused in return. I had to forgive my doctors, as well.

While I was hospitalized during one episode, my new doctor told me he was releasing me from his care. I remember crying out to God, fighting off the feelings of discouragement and the suicidal thoughts that had once again returned. No one could help me, and the pain was intolerable. *Why was God not healing me? I believed! I loved God! I forgave! I went to healing services! I did all the right things!*

I felt as if God had totally abandoned me. Toward the end of my quest for deliverance, after suffering nine years in tortuous pain, every day was spent lying perfectly still staring at the ceiling. I could not read or watch TV. I could not move because every breath or slight movement was like a razor scraping all the nerves in my spine. I got up only a couple of times a day to use the bathroom. That was my life for almost three years. *What was God trying to tell me?* I still believed He was there and that He loved me, but hadn't I suffered enough?

In hindsight, I could not see the transformation in my soul. I offer this analogy: An earthquake strikes in some part of the world. Poor, suffering people are buried beneath the rubble. Rescue workers come and carefully begin lifting brick by brick, stone by stone, so as not to cause further collapse or harm. The buried person may have no idea that boulders are being lifted, but the saving work is in progress.

The same is true for us. Sometimes, the damage is so severe that God, in His wisdom, carefully and skillfully lifts burden by burden, binding wound upon wound until we are able to receive and handle the gift of healing. God *was* healing me, but the process needed to be slower than I wanted so that no further damage would be done. I was on such a self-destructive path because of the rage deep within me; instant healing would have been dangerous.

God worked miracles on my way to healing. My son stopped using drugs cold turkey and never went back. My daughter had come back home; I was not completely alone anymore. My youngest son and

I were able to buy a small house, so I could be on one floor instead of in an unsafe three-story apartment. Friends were slowly making appearances. Relationships were healing.

As I reflected on my journey, I knew God had been hard at work—molding me, transforming me, strengthening me. I was becoming patient and peaceful. I was learning about God and myself, as well as what was really of value. I was becoming deeply compassionate and forgiving. The life of the Risen Christ was residing in me, and I was not the same person anymore. I began to be an encourager to others.

I remember when a chaplain talked to me as I lay in a hospital bed for a second week of testing, which would still provide no answers. As he left, he said, "Sister, you have ministered to me when I was supposed to minister to you. Where did you get this faith? Please consider this experience an invitation from God to follow this path and help others in their suffering!"

The most wonderful thing of all was that Jesus was wooing me. That relationship became more precious to me than any earthly thing. I used to joke with Him, telling Him that falling in love with another man would be impossible because He was becoming everything I had ever dreamed of. I felt God was calling me to Himself; I became a consecrated widow, similar to a religious sister except I live in the world and not in a religious community. I made vows of chastity, obedience, and simplicity in my state of life.

One of my fellow consecrated widows brought me Holy Communion one particular afternoon when I was very discouraged. I remember her saying, "God will never leave His servants hanging. Cling to hope because if you give that up, the devil will have you. He doesn't want you to be able to do the work God has planned for you. Say, 'Get behind me, Satan, for God is before me!'" I felt a huge spiritual battle inside me, but I thanked God for sending me strong, faithful people to lift me up when I could not lift myself.

Though my condition was worsening, God was blessing me with many spiritual experiences. My time alone was a time of great grace. I was growing in love and relationship with God and learning who I was in Christ. I was learning about each person of the Trinity as persons, as friends. I was entering a love like I had never known.

For the first time in my adult life, I felt safe, protected, loved, treasured, reverenced, respected. These feelings were unfamiliar to me. I felt a dignity in being part of this Family and participating in this gift of love. As the wounds of my heart were being tended, I was coming closer to the healing I desired.

Around 3:00 p.m. on August 9, 2012, my pain level was so high that I could not go on anymore. I had given birth to three children naturally and with very hard labors, yet this suffering was far beyond what I had experienced. My local doctors continued to misdiagnose the problems in my back and hips. The suffering was inhuman, and I felt myself slipping away.

Here is an excerpt from my journal that day:

I feel like I am being dragged into hell. I simply took a breath and could feel the scraping of the raw nerve endings once again. I feel like my body is going to give out, like I am ready to die. My body can't take this anymore. Please, Jesus, have mercy.

I trust You. I praise You. I love You. I thank You. I will not fear. Even if I have to descend into the pit again, then that will be heaven for me because You will be there with me. If these are my last words to you, Jesus, then let them be "Jesus, I trust in you."

I obviously did not die that afternoon but woke the next day with total peace. I realized Satan no longer has power over us when we allow Christ to enter our suffering and transform it. Maybe God was healing one component of my suffering: fear.

Three days later, God moved things into place, and my help was finally coming. I had decided that I would rather be helpless in His arms than in control on my own. On August 12, 2012, I prayed differently: *Jesus, I surrender all to your control. I choose to let go of control and trust you.*

In order to catch monkeys, African hunters bait them into putting their hand into a small hole and grabbing a jar of food. When the monkey grabs it, he has a dilemma: If he does not let go of the jar, he cannot escape. The monkey could drop the food and easily get his hand out, but he will not. Instead, he will hold the food until the hunter captures it. I was that poor creature: All I needed to do was let go, and I could have been free. I kept myself trapped when I refused to let go.

Jesus, I trust in you. Those words I thought would be my last unlocked the floodgates of heaven. Trusting in Him and finally letting go of control allowed the miracles to begin.

One day, out of the blue, a physical therapist called. She and I rarely talked, but that day she said, "Tammy, I just saw a patient who had severe back issues like yours, and she just returned from a doctor in New Jersey. Her recovery is so remarkable that I felt I had to call you and give you the contact information."

So many disappointing and frustrating dealings with doctors had jaded me; my first thought was to humor her, thank her, and not follow up. Fear began to wash over me, but I instantly felt Jesus's presence, even before I began to pray. My Jesus rushed to help when I was being attacked. The Holy Spirit moved in me, and I picked up the phone with an unexplainable boldness and hope. I was not going to give up: What if this was the miracle I prayed for?

The following day, my friend's father was at my house, and when I told him about a potential doctor, he helped me gather my health records and tests to send to New Jersey. Though I could not do the simple task myself, God sent someone who could.

The next day, Satan tormented me with thoughts of discouragement: "You're going to be disappointed again. You know no one can help you. Your case is hopeless." I refused to listen. I sang songs to Jesus and prayed through the day and night.

On August 15, the feast of the Assumption, my first miracle happened. On this feast, Catholics commemorate when Jesus's Mother was taken to Heaven. I took this as a sign. Around 1:00 p.m., the doctor in New Jersey called. I had been treated so poorly from the local doctors that I was in disbelief. This doctor, who had been so concerned about my case, had even called me on his way home from his vacation in China. He returned the next day, and once he saw my medical records and MRIs, he said he could help me. I was thrilled. Was my deliverance finally here?

When I calmed down, I realized I did not have the necessary insurance to afford the $10,000 surgery, nor did I have a way to get to New Jersey. In such bad shape, I could not travel by plane or car, but my faith had become so strong. I believed without a doubt that if Jesus wanted me to have the surgery, these problems would resolve. I began thanking Jesus for what He was going to do.

I remember my charismatic priest friend came to pray over me. As he sat on my couch the following day, I shared all that had transpired. When I told him I believed Jesus was going to provide the money, he was in disbelief. He shook his head, saying, "Be realistic! Ten thousand dollars? This can't be. Another back surgery would be so dangerous. Look what happened with the last two."

But nothing was going to shake my belief. "If God wants me to have this surgery, that money is going to come."

At that very moment, a friend and fellow parishioner who heard of my situation pulled into my driveway with a check for that exact amount. The priest was flabbergasted.

As I waited the three weeks until my surgery date, a few priest friends came to pray with me, as did a few different prayer groups from various faiths. Catholic or Protestant, we were all brothers and sisters in Christ and loved each other in Christian unity, just as Jesus had prayed "that they may all be one" (John 17:21). The pain and waiting were hard, and I was thankful for the prayer support.

But the day before the trip, my ride cancelled. My friend who owned a van had volunteered to drive me to New Jersey, so I could make the trip lying down. I prayed and then called the parish priest. As I was telling him, an elderly couple, Cat and Jim O'Brien, overheard the conversation and offered to drive me. God knew they would be the perfect ones to help me; I would need a woman's help as I recovered.

After the surgery, Dr. Liu told me that the damage from my first surgery was extensive. My first surgeon butchered me; excessive scar tissue and many adhesions were choking and pulling on the nerves. Though Dr. Liu saw other problems that might have needed addressing, he said I should have relief within two weeks.

The next few months showed some improvement, but I was still in severe pain and very limited. Still not understanding God's ways, I was expecting a total cure immediately. When I did not get it, discouragement set in. In His goodness, God sent help.

As I was falling into self-pity, the story of Joni Eareckson Tada, who became a quadriplegic after she suffered a diving injury, was on the radio. I was deeply moved and inspired. This woman faced more hardships than I and yet used every one to give glory to God and bring others to Him.

The Bible tells us, "We are afflicted in every way, but not crushed; perplexed, but not driven to despair; persecuted, but not forsaken; struck down, but not destroyed; always carrying in the body the death of Jesus, so that the life of Jesus may also be manifested in our bodies" (2 Cor. 4:8–18). In her story, I learned the enemy will always try to divert us from hope and healing and will always be there with negativity and lies. However, we can either listen to the darkness that will only destroy us, or we can choose to trust God.

The following May, Dr. Liu suggested addressing the other problems he had seen in my first surgery; I would need five surgeries in all. During the drive, the pain became so overwhelming that I thought I was going to faint. Then, I felt a presence with me as I lay in the back seat. Prior to this trip, I had no real knowledge or devotion to St. Padre Pio, but I truly believe he came to me during that trip. He asked me to pray a rosary with him, and I began the first few prayers. The next thing I knew, we were at the hospital. We had been only a third of the way into this six-hour drive. I am usually an analytical, factual, logical person; however, Padre Pio's presence was unexplainable.

The Book of Revelation speaks about the "cloud of witnesses": "An angel came and stood at the altar with a golden censer; and he was given much incense to mingle with the prayers of all the saints upon the golden altar before the throne; and the smoke of the incense rose with the prayers of the saints from the hand of the angel before God" (Rev. 8:3–4). Though some may think I was simply hallucinating from the pain, this former Protestant who had no real exposure to saints discovered that God can use the Body of Christ both on earth and in Heaven to help us.

My allergy to opiates meant controlling pain during surgery would be a challenge. The anesthesia did not work; in this procedure that involved a hammer, a steel rod, and a drill, I felt everything—a tiny glimpse of Jesus's experience as He was nailed to the cross. After the surgery, Dr. Liu explained the damage had been much more extensive than expected. Tissue and nerves were growing like tentacles around my discs; in his twenty years of practice, he had never seen anything like it.

As the days after surgery wore on, I noticed a tiny bit of relief, but something was still seriously wrong. As one layer of my pain was fixed, the true root of the problem was now becoming more evident. I was so worn out from suffering. Why was my healing miracle taking so long? Dr. Liu graciously called me at home to check up on me and told me other surgeries needed to be done before deeper issues could be addressed. I pressed on.

I reluctantly saw a local physical therapist at the suggestion of my primary care doctor. The physical therapist discovered the root of the problem in five minutes. Shocked and angry with myself for having been too stubborn to listen to that suggestion ten years earlier, I wondered if I had been contributing to my own misery.

But God knew best, and I kept repeating, "God will do the most loving thing in the most loving way for the greatest amount of good." God had known I was not ready to be physically healed, so He worked with my stubbornness to heal me in a better way—from the inside out. As Scripture says, "We know that God causes all things to work together for good to those who love God, to those who are called according to His purpose" (Rom. 8:28). God worked everything for my good, even when I was wrong. His love was bigger than my mistakes.

Over the next six months, my physical therapist and Dr. Liu worked together to get me into a study so that the next two surgeries that would repair my sacroiliac (SI) joints in my hips would be free. My SI joints were "floppy," as my PT used to joke with me, remarking that the ligaments in that area were like Jell-O, completely unable to hold the joints in place. Without a good foundation, my back suffered, too. So much damage had been done because I was misdiagnosed for so long (ten years and twelve doctors, not including hospitalizations).

In December 2013, I had two more surgeries, and my pain level dropped so significantly that I hobbled out of the hospital taking little more than Tylenol. The pain relief was instantaneous. Though not in the way or timeframe I had expected, God came through.

As I began the new year, I was beginning to live again. When we are stripped of important things, every step, every morsel of food, every

sight and sound become reminders of our humanity and our dependence on God. I walked to my mailbox and wept with joy. I began to
play music again at church; the first time I picked up my guitar again,
the tears flowed. My children benefitted, and healing within our family
was another source of joy and thanksgiving. After learning of all that
my mother had suffered, I better understood her inability to fully love
me. I began to truly love her, and we now have a beautiful relationship.
And as my physical therapist helped me in my post-surgical rehab, she
also became my friend. God had clearly orchestrated this relationship
because, at that point in her life, she needed me as much as I needed
her.

During Holy Week of 2015, my final and most difficult surgery
took place. During the eight-and-a-half-hour surgery, I was cut from
the front, as well as the back. Due to my intolerance to pain medication,
I had a massive allergic reaction that caused weeping hives all over my
abdomen and back. Every time I moved post-surgery, the hospital
gown would pull away from the scabs, reopening the oozing wounds.
My right leg was paralyzed, so I could not reposition myself and had to
wait for help. I was very sick and in excruciating pain, but pain medication would cause vomiting and the allergy to worsen.

One afternoon, as I lay in my own blood and pus, my monthly
cycle came with such force I thought I was hemorrhaging and was helpless to do anything to alleviate my misery.

As the church bells down the street rang, I wished I could experience the Holy Week services. In reality, I was sharing in His Passion
more than I realized. I could not sleep or pray. Despite the horrible
suffering and the realization that I might be paralyzed, I had a deep
peace, knowing Jesus was present and in control. Just as Jesus had
overcome sin and death on the very first Good Friday, I had overcome
the enemy's attempts to destroy me and turn me away from God. How
sweet the victory! I let go completely of the distorted self-sufficiency
that brought me to that state and was completely resigned to His will.

As the Easter Vigil Mass began, I longed to be there but praised
God right there on my bed of pain anyway. Suddenly, my leg moved
slightly. I yelled for the nurse. There was hope! Overwhelmed, I hardly
slept that night.

On Easter morning, only a few days after a surgery in which all of my core muscles had been cut, I felt energy surge through my body and stood up unassisted. The nurse commanded me to lie down, but I would not listen. I was screaming, "I am healed! I can walk!" With the physical therapist following closely behind me, I walked up and down the halls wishing everyone a happy Easter and telling them how great God is. I had received a miracle that Easter morning. God had held me up and carried me through my own Way of the Cross.

I wish I could say the next few days were easy. Getting on a plane and being delayed at the airport for three hours with very little pain medicine was torture. Only by the grace of God did I get home. The hives continued for six months, but I was on my way. God had brought me through the most debilitating, tortuous years of my life. Not only did I survive; I overcame! God transformed what the enemy meant for harm into a period of growth, awakening, and victory.

I would like to share in the next chapters the valuable information I learned in the healing process. I hope something here helps you achieve the breakthrough you seek.

As for you, you meant evil against me but God meant it for good in order to bring about this present result, to preserve many people alive.
(Gen. 50:20)

Jesus, I trust in You!

CHAPTER 2

What It Means to Be Healed

If there's no breaking, then there's no healing,
and if there's no healing, then there's no learning.
-One Tree Hill

W hat father among you, if his son asks for a fish, will instead of a fish give him a serpent; or if he asks for an egg, will give him a scorpion? If you then, who are evil, know how to give good gifts to your children, how much more will the heavenly Father give the Holy Spirit to those who ask him!" (Luke 11:11–13).

None of us would want to watch our child, spouse, parent, or pet suffer. Instead, we want the best for them. God loves us as any good parent loves his or her child, even more so because He is perfect love. However, a good parent sometimes allows a child to experience bumps and bruises. Likewise, God does not promise that we will be spared suffering, but He does promise to be with us and bring good out of it. As Romans tells us, "And we know that God causes all things to work together for good to those who love God" (Rom. 8:28).

Healing as "Wholeness"

Merriam-Webster defines healing as "the process of making or becoming sound or whole again." The root of the word *healing* in the New Testament Greek, *sozo*, is the same as that of *salvation* and *wholeness*. We are body, soul, and spirit; to truly heal, we may need work on more than one of these at a time. For example, we can receive a physical healing yet still not be "whole." We may think the healing we need is a simple fix, but God wants "wholeness," which might require a different method than what we expect. Published by the Congregation for the Doctrine of the Faith, the *Instruction on Prayers for Healing* states, "The meeting between Christ and the sick, is to heal the person in his or her totality, and hence with a dimension of eternity. Sickness is an evil. People are called to joy. Nevertheless, each day they experience many forms of suffering and pain. Therefore, the Lord, in his promises of redemption, announces the joy of the heart that comes from liberation from sufferings"[1]. Thus, the Church affirms that sickness is an evil and that God wants us to be joyful and healed.

Satan uses sickness, disease, and death to bind, oppress, and prevent us from having the good that God wants for us. The evil one wants us to believe that God does not care, that God wants us to suffer, or that God is punishing us. But God hates suffering, as Christ shows us countless times in the Gospels: "And Jesus went about all the cities and villages, teaching in their synagogues and preaching the gospel of the kingdom, and healing every disease and every infirmity. When he saw the crowds, *he had compassion for them*, because they were harassed and helpless, like sheep without a shepherd" (Matt. 9:35).

His heart is nothing but compassion, and God desires us to be well and whole. The *Catechism of the Catholic Church* stresses that "Christ's compassion toward the sick and his many healings of every kind of infirmity are a resplendent sign that 'God has visited his people' and that the kingdom of God is close at hand. Jesus has the power not only to heal, but also to forgive sins; he has come to heal the whole man, soul and body; he is the physician the sick have need of" (CCC 1503).

"Wholeness": The Body, Soul, Spirit Connection

As I was nearing the end of my healing journey, I was subconsciously doubting God, doubting the therapists that God had provided, and doubting my body's ability to heal. During one particular session of craniosacral therapy after my successful surgeries, I was pleading with the therapist to help me with the dizziness and back pain that still remained. She, like my other health providers, said my problem was now in the deeper tissues of the brain and nervous system, not simply in the muscles or bones. Jesus Himself had been telling me in prayer that my back was healed, but because my back still hurt, I stubbornly did not believe it.

As the therapist worked on my head, I heard Jesus say, "The pain is coming from your head"; within seconds, the therapist spoke those exact words. She told me that my pain and other issues now were in the dura. Still in doubt, I asked God to confirm what she was saying. Suddenly, as she touched an area of my head, my back pain soared; she moved to my lower back, and the dizziness skyrocketed. It was all connected: The pain was indeed coming from the dura, the lining of the brain and spinal cord.

As I lay there praying, memories of past abuse began to surface for no reason, and I began to weep. As if a cover were being removed, I could see clearly my lack of trust in God, others, and even myself. Jesus was showing me that my emotional wounds were impacting my physical health. I began to let go of the past hurts and fears, which I had no idea still existed, and opened myself to trusting the gifts flowing from God's heart of mercy and love. I began to accept that God was working through these medical professionals; the light of Jesus was truly flowing through my body, allowing it to heal. After the session, I significantly improved not only physically but emotionally and spiritually, too. My relationship with God grew that day, and I became a firm believer that the human person is truly an integration of body, soul and spirit (1 Thess. 5:23).

The Integration of Faith and Medicine

Although God does desire us to be well, a miracle cure and healing are two different concepts. Miracles are usually instantaneous with no natural explanation. Healing, on the other hand, is generally a gradual process of repair, regeneration, and regrowth over time. It is not a spiritual slot machine where God grants our wishes, only if we say the right combination of prayers; God is also not a Santa Claus figure who fulfills every desire on our wish list. (What a narrow, one-sided relationship if we view Him this way!) Though complete healing might be the end goal, the journey is just as important and is often a positive, blessed experience. We must be careful not to dictate to God the healing method we feel would be best.

The Gospel of John says, "When He had said this, He spat on the ground, and made clay of the spittle, and applied the clay to his eyes, and said to him, 'Go, wash in the pool of Siloam' (which is translated, 'Sent'). So he went away and washed, and came back seeing" (John 9:6–8). In this miracle, the omnipotent Jesus did not *need* to use a resource (the clay) to heal, but He did so to show that He can make use of any person or substance to bring about his will. Those who minister healing, whether physical or spiritual, become channels of God's love. Even though God (not the instrument He chooses) is the one who heals, God sometimes does use His creation to effect healing. Therefore, we must be open to whatever method God employs to bring about our healing.

Many believe either doctors or prayer, one or the other, will provide healing. However, seeking help from a prayer ministry in no way detracts from the gifts God gives through medicine and other therapies. Prayer is not a substitute for medicine or maintaining one's health. Both add to our total resources for wholeness. Thus, we bear some responsibility for our healing. We cannot ask God to cure our health issue and refuse to follow our doctor's advice. We must cooperate with God, and we must be open to the process. Some may be afraid to go to the doctors because of what they might find; some fear the unknown or that the cure might hurt. Without trust, we cannot heal; we must give ourselves completely to the Divine Physician and allow Him to treat us.

In the book *Padre Pio: The True Story* by C. Bernard Ruffin[2], Padre Pio, who was widely known for having the gift of healing, was adamant that a dying woman, Amealia Abresch, go to a hospital to be healed. Many wondered why he did not heal her himself. Padre Pio insisted, "People think I have miracles. I have no miracles. If you think you have received a grace, go to Our Lord and thank Him. Not me!" Padre Pio respected God's sovereignty and knew he did not possess the gift of healing. God worked through him as He saw fit. Padre Pio reminds us not make a person, or a healing ministry, our god, and we should not try to tell God how He should heal us.

But Why Does It Have to Take So Long?

During my many years of suffering, I wanted desperately for God to heal me instantly, though I later realized the blessings and graces of God's timetable. One such blessing from God's "delayed" timing was that others benefitted from my experience. Besides my education as a registered nurse, God led me to be trained in "complementary" healing—nutrition, body mechanics, craniosacral therapy, facial release, the use of essential oils and herbs, and more. Though not the instant cures I sought, these modalities brought some relief to my unrelenting suffering; they were the "Simon of Cyrene" that helped me through the most tortuous years of my life. My knowledge of these modalities helped many others on their way to healing; similarly, God often uses our present trials to touch others and be lights on their journeys because we understand what they are going through.

Moreover, we are sometimes so deeply wounded that God must heal us slowly so as to bring about a total restoration. In the earthquake example in chapter 1, rescue workers lift one stone at a time off a buried person, who is often unaware that the work is being done. Sometimes, our internal, emotional, or spiritual damage is so severe that God, in His wisdom, carefully lifts burden by burden. He binds wound upon wound until we are able to receive and handle the gift of healing.

Again, God will do the most loving thing in the most loving way for the greatest amount of good. Healing is one of the many gifts of God's love, and He promises us countless times through scripture that our suffering will end. My prayer is that you will find the answers you seek and that I can offer advice to help in the meantime. In the next chapter, as we try to get to know our God better, we will look at His Word and what He says about healing.

In the World, you will have tribulation but take courage;
I have overcome the world. (John 16:33 [NASB])

Jesus, I trust that You want to help me.

CHAPTER 3

Healing in Scripture

Ignorance of Scripture is ignorance of Christ.
-St. Jerome

I recently watched a TV show about a stray dog. A rescue worker sat down near the poor animal—who was frightened, hungry, and injured—and offered it food. It was too frightened to move, so the rescuer patiently waited for the dog to respond. Finally, the poor animal's desire to alleviate its hunger pains outweighed its fear and suspicion, and it slowly crept near the worker, grabbed the food, and retreated.

All too often, we treat God the same way. When we are in need, we plead with God and play a spiritual game of "Let's Make a Deal." When He comes to our rescue, we say a quick "thanks" and go on with life until the next crisis hits. He tenderly and lovingly comes to our rescue and meets us where we are; we respond by taking what we want from Him before retreating to our same misery.

Eventually, the dog learned to trust the rescue worker, and their bond became so strong that the worker adopted the dog. Similarly, God is there to rescue us, to be that best friend; He will never walk away or stop loving us.

We may doubt whether God is really good, whether He is holding out on us, whether He really cares about the happenings in our lives, whether He truly wants to help. So often, we project our human weaknesses and shortcomings on God. In order to understand how God wants good for us and wants to see us happy and healed, we must turn to the place where we can truly get to know Him: Scripture.

The Importance of Scripture

The Gospel of John begins, "In the beginning was the Word, and the Word was with God, and the Word was God. He was in the beginning with God. All things came into being through Him, and apart from Him nothing came into being that has come into being" (John 1:1–3). The Word of God is creative and powerful because God *is* the Word.

The Bible tells us many times about the importance of the Word. St. Paul calls the Word "the sword of the Spirit" and tells us to take it up as we put on the "full armor of God" (Eph. 6:11, 17). Hebrews says "the word of God is living and active and sharper than any two-edged sword . . . able to judge the thoughts and intentions of the heart" (Heb. 4:12 [NASB]). Jesus Himself says, "If you abide in Me, and My words abide in you, ask whatever you wish, and it will be done for you" (John 15:7 [NASB]).

God wants us to know His Word because we will find Him in it. Because the Word is so vitally important, I have included some Scripture verses related to healing in the appendix of this book; they may be used as a reference and source of encouragement. However, we will also delve into Scripture now to better understand the heart and will of God as we seek healing.

God Wills Our Good

We are all familiar with the Lord's Prayer, but how often do we truly reflect on the words? Jesus tells us to pray, "Thy kingdom come. Thy will be done on earth as it is in Heaven."

What will Heaven be like? What does God's Kingdom look like to you? Take a moment to jot down immediately what comes to mind: Do you think of peace? happiness? time spent with those you loved on earth? Are you filled with excitement at the thought of meeting God? Do you picture an eternity with no pain, with no suffering?

When God's kingdom is preached in Scripture, there is wholeness and healing. Before the fall, everything existed to give glory to God; every creature lived, not for his own glory, but for God's. Sin destroyed God's kingdom on earth. Not desiring God's will for us led to a life of misery. While God wanted us to be healthy, happy, and satisfied—a life of perfect love—the lack of trust and a focus on the self took Adam and Eve, and thus us, out of Eden.

The Kingdom of God is about more than the removal of trial, hardship, pain, or injury; it instead undoes the damage done by our human will. It leads us to wholeness and back into will of our Father.

Throughout the Gospels, Jesus speaks about the Kingdom and healing together.

- "And as you go, preach, saying, 'The *kingdom* of heaven is at hand.' *Heal* the sick, cleanse the lepers, raise the dead, cast out demons. Freely you have received, freely give." (Matt. 10:7–8 [NASB])
- "Whatever city you enter and they receive you, eat what is set before you; and *heal* those in it who are sick, and say to them, 'The *kingdom* of God has come near to you.'" (Luke 10: 8–9 [NASB])
- "He began speaking to them about the *kingdom* of God and curing those who had need of *healing*." (Luke 9:11 [NASB])

Thus, we know that suffering and sickness are absent in Heaven. If we want God's kingdom to come "on earth as it is in Heaven," Jesus wants us to be free and whole here, too.

Friendship with God

In the Gospel of Mark, "a leper came to him and kneeling down begged him and said, 'If you wish, you can make me clean.' Moved with pity, [Jesus] stretched out his hand, touched him, and said to him, '*I do will it*. Be made clean'" (Mark 1:40–41 [NASB]).

God is moved with pity! When He sees us suffering, His heart aches *for* us and *with* us—a sign of someone who truly loves us. His heart is compassion, and the aim of His will is love. This love cannot be one sided; instead, He calls us to a relationship with Him.

In Exodus, when Moses is on the mountain receiving the Ten Commandments, God wants to destroy the Israelites in their camp. Moses pleads with God, who relents. God changes His mind when Moses asks Him because "the Lord used to speak to Moses face to face, *as a man speaks to his friend*" (Exod. 33:11 [RSVCE]). They had a relationship; they were friends!

With those closest to us, we talk regularly, hug, laugh, and share our feelings and dreams. Because of these interactions, a strong bond forms, and trust develops. A relationship is secured. Should our relationship with God, who is completely in love with us, be any different? God wants us to come to Him and talk as a friend would. Just like a true friend responds in haste to our needs, God is here for us when we need Him.

Likewise, we see Jesus develop a friendship with Martha and Mary and their brother, Lazarus. He taught them, ate with them, and loved them ("Jesus loved Martha and her sister and Lazarus" [John 11:5]). I like to picture them praying with each other, staying up late at night just to chat, and sharing jokes and heartaches.

When Lazarus dies, the Gospel tells us, "Jesus wept" (John 11:35). Of course, He did! His good friend, whom He loved, had died. In their affliction, Martha and Mary turn to Him and trust that He has the power to do wonderful things. He knew they believed and trusted in Him; in turn, He does not want His friends to feel pain and loss. Because of that love and relationship, Jesus is able to perform the incredible miracle of raising Lazarus from the dead.

Picturing sitting and chatting with Jesus on a warm evening while crickets chirp and the stars shine above is easy. But when God allows pain in our lives, do we still trust Him, or do we angrily turn away? If we believe that Jesus is our true friend and we are in a true relationship with Him, we have to trust in Him as we would any friend; such trust is foundational to our healing. Jesus wants our wills to be united, to be our true friend. His will is always the best possible thing for us.

His Will, His Way, His Timing

Now Peter and John were going up to the temple at the ninth hour, the hour of prayer. And a man who had been lame from his mother's womb was being carried along, whom they used to set down every day at the gate of the temple, which is called Beautiful, in order to beg alms of those who were entering the temple. When he saw Peter and John about to go into the temple, he began asking to receive alms. But Peter, along with John, fixed his gaze on him and said, "Look at us!" And he began to give them his attention, expecting to receive something from them. But Peter said, "I do not possess silver and gold, but what I do have I give to you: In the name of Jesus Christ the Nazarene—walk!" And seizing him by the right hand, he raised him up; and immediately his feet and his ankles were strengthened. With a leap he stood upright and began to walk; and he entered the temple with them, walking and leaping and praising God. And all the people saw him walking and praising God; and they were taking note of him as being the one who used to sit at the Beautiful Gate of the temple to beg alms, and they were filled with wonder and amazement at what had happened to him. (Acts 3:1–10 [NASB])

The man was at the gate every day since birth. Jesus went to the temple often, so Jesus likely walked by without curing Him. Although Scripture does not explicitly explain why not, some say Jesus did not heal the man who seemed more focused on alms than on healing. For us, this passage invites us to ask, "Am I holding on too tightly to a belief, relationship, or desire when there is something more that Jesus offers me? Is there a fear or discomfort that keeps me from moving forward?"

Maybe God had a bigger plan for this beggar. Did Jesus not heal the man Himself because He had a plan to bring about a greater good according to His perfect timing? God ordained Peter, the leader of the new Christian Church, to bring about this healing in His name and to demonstrate the power God gives to His Bride, the Church. Peter also said to the beggar, "Look at us"; knowing the Holy Spirit was prompting him to perform this miracle, Peter wanted the man to be fully aware of the source of his healing. God's desire was for the man to be whole; though his healing did not happen in the way people expected, God in His perfect will, in His perfect wisdom, did it in His perfect time.

In a different story, a man with little faith cries out to Jesus to heal his possessed son: "'But if You can do anything, take pity on us and help us!' And Jesus said to him, "'If You can?" All things are possible to him who believes.' Immediately the boy's father cried out and said, 'I do believe; help my unbelief'" (Mark 9:22–24 [NASB]).

Here is a man with little faith, but Jesus challenges him to delve deeper and then works the miracle to cure his son. Jesus took what little faith the man had and helped it grow.

Here is another story from the Gospel of John:

> Now there is in Jerusalem by the sheep gate a pool, which is called in Hebrew Bethesda, having five porticoes. In these lay a multitude of those who were sick, blind, lame, and withered, waiting for the moving of the waters; for an angel of the Lord went down at certain seasons into the pool and stirred up the water; whoever then first, after the stirring up of the water, stepped in was made well from whatever disease with which he was afflicted. A man was there who had been ill for thirty-eight years. When Jesus saw him lying there, and knew that he had already been a long time in that condition, He said to him, "Do you wish to get well?" The sick man answered Him, "Sir, I have no man to put me into the pool when the water is stirred up, but while I am coming, another steps down before me." Jesus said to him, "Get up, pick up your pallet and walk." Immediately the man became well, and picked up his pallet and began to walk. (John 5:2–9 [NASB])

Amid all of the sick at the pool, Jesus was drawn to this poor man who had been waiting for thirty-eight years. He must have felt frustrated, desperate, and helpless. He probably felt abandoned by everyone, including God. How surprised he must have been when Jesus asks him, "Do you wish to get well?"

Like the man in the story, I had been sick for a long time—eleven years, at this point—and was bedridden for a good part of it. Like the man, I also had my doubts. *Is God's will for me to suffer? Will I ever be healed? Is God giving up on me, just like these doctors have?*

I was shocked when a doctor asked me the same question: "Do you wish to be well?"

I responded, "Of course, I do!"

The doctor, like Jesus, gave me instructions. Though I was not instantly restored as the invalid was, this moment was another step in my faith that ultimately led to my healing. Jesus was speaking through the doctor that day, calling me to a higher level of faith. I have since found that praying "According to your perfect will" rather than "*If* it is your will" emanates trust and radical confidence in our loving God, rather than projecting doubt that God wants us to be healed.

In a world of instant gratification, waiting often feels like the end of the world. My time as both a nurse and a member of prayer ministries has shown me that God can heal instantly, but I have also witnessed people who are healed only after years of praying and waiting. I have heard that "healing sometimes requires a scalpel, but even that can be merciful—to cut away what is unnecessary and spare what is good." Trust that God knows what He is doing, even if the process hurts. As Scripture teaches us, God does have a perfect plan for us and wills our good; sometimes that perfect Will, which requires wholehearted trust from us, requires us to find the beauty in the waiting.

You did not choose Me but I chose you, and appointed you that you would go and bear fruit, and that your fruit would remain, so that whatever you ask of the Father in My name He may give to you. (John 15:16)

Jesus, I trust that You want me to be whole.

CHAPTER 4

On Waiting

The only thing harder than waiting on God is wishing you had.
-Steven Furtick

When a website takes more than a few seconds to load, we groan with frustration. Christmas begins in October, sex is expected on the third date, and we want to be a CEO right out of college. Impatience and instant gratification dominate modern attitudes, and we do not even realize we are robbed of the joy of anticipation.

Joyce Meyer said, "Patience is not simply the ability to wait—it's how we behave while we're waiting."[1] To wait on the Lord is active, not passive, like we tend to believe. We anticipate and watch for God to move or for us to move at His direction. Yet most of us still need to learn how to wait on the Lord.

When God asks us to wait, we complain, asking why He is taking so long; we get impatient when we do not see the results we are expecting right away. We want to take matters into our own hands and, often, unnecessarily make things worse. We miss the point of God's wisdom in asking us to wait for Him.

As a Type A personality, I found waiting to be impossible. I was a doer, a problem solver for the world, so learning to trust someone else was difficult. I felt like nothing was getting done, that God was not doing anything. But God *was* working, and the more still I became, the more he seemed to do. Mountains that seemed immovable were now mere pebbles. The more I trusted He knew what He was doing, that He could do what I could not, situations changed for the better.

Waiting and Silence

The word "wait" is used over one hundred times in the Bible. Isaiah says, "They who wait for the Lord shall renew their strength" (Isa. 40:31). When we wait, we renew our strength as we tire from the struggle to "let go and let God."

Waiting upon the Lord requires silence and stillness. Psalm 46 tells us, "Be still and know that I am God" (Ps. 46:10). With the overabundance of noise and distraction in our lives—TV or radio as background noise, smartphones compulsively checked every five minutes, even ads while we are filling up our gas tanks—finding silence is difficult.

However, silence brings rest, and rest indicates trust. We must push aside thoughts that we are wasting our time and instead be unafraid to be silent before Him. When we are silent, we come face-to-face with our deepest selves. When we quietly rest in His presence, an enveloping warmth of communion with our Heavenly Father leaves a transformative imprint on our souls.

Near the very end of my period of waiting on God, a friend visited. After watching me for a while, she exclaimed, "I can't believe it! You, of all people, have learned to be still and quiet." For the first time in my life, I was a newborn baby, content and satisfied resting in my Father's arms. I did not need TV, noise, or distraction. Only through learning the richness of waiting in silence did I come to understand its beauty.

Just as Mary waited before the Holy Spirit overshadowed her, waiting on God leads to expectation and hope. We can be so self-reliant at times, but in allowing ourselves to surrender and wait, we experience the security of depending on our powerful God who loves us more than we could imagine. When we wait, we are transformed and see movements of God we were unable to see before. We learn to trust that God has a plan and purpose, that He has good reasons for making us wait.

Waiting patiently can

- reveal our true motives, hidden sins, and idols.
- help us grow in patience and other virtues.
- foster a sense of appreciation and make our eventual outcomes more valuable.
- build character.
- open the way to deeper intimacy with God in our total dependence on Him.
- reveal the hearts of those in our lives who may not stand beside us in our struggles.
- help us gain a clearer perspective and diffuse emotions to get to the bigger issue.
- be an opportunity to savor the present moment and all its blessings.

Waiting in Scripture

The Bible is full of stories of waiting. When we look at familiar Bible characters who were told to wait, we can see why God chooses to make his people wait.

1. *Abraham and Sarah*: God promised Abraham and Sarah a child. Waiting so many years with no children proved too much, so Abraham conceived a child with Hagar, Sarah's slave. They failed to believe that God could do the miraculous; waiting revealed their lack of trust, their self-sufficiency, and eventually Sarah's jealously. Do we produce Ishmaels when we cannot wait for God to give us our Isaacs? Do we try to grasp by our own efforts rather than wait to receive the gift from God's hands? (Gen. 18:1–15)

2. *Joseph Imprisoned*: Joseph was sold into slavery and later imprisoned. Twenty-one years later, his brothers and father came back to him as he was made prince of Egypt. The jour-

ney from pit to throne was a long journey of trust, but through Joseph's difficulty and waiting, God saved him and his entire family. Do we let our light shine, even in our trials? (Gen. 30–50)

3. *The Woman with the Issue of Blood*: A woman had been suffering from a blood issue for twelve years. Determined, she pressed through to reach Jesus, exercising her faith and receiving healing. Do we give up too easily, or do we press through, no matter what, to make contact with Him? (Mark 5:21–34)

4. *Lazarus's Rising from the Dead*: Lazarus had been dead for four days when Jesus arrived. Jesus used this miracle—and the time He made Martha and Mary wait—to show them something about believing in who He is and in hoping in Him when difficulties seem impossible. Do we believe God is the God of impossible situations? Do we see Christ, or do we see only the problem in front of us? (John 11:1–44)

5. *The Man at Bethesda*: An invalid man waited thirty-eight years, arriving every day with no real hope of getting into the pool to be healed. Jesus asked him, "Do you wish to be healed?" Perhaps this question was a chance to see if the man had any hope left; God can do so much with so little. Do we give in to despair—a sign that we do not believe that God is worthy of our trust? (John 5:1–15)

6. *The Man at the Gate Beautiful*: Lame from birth, this man must have been so discouraged when Jesus passed by him day after day; maybe he was fearful of how different his life would be if he were healed. Jesus may have been waiting for the man to fully believe and receive, and the Bible tells us the man's healing came "that the works of God may be displayed in him." Do we find ourselves afraid of the future or what will be expected of us if we are healed? Are we open to whatever method of healing God chooses? (Acts 3:1–9)

7. *The Kingship of David*: David waited over twenty years for God's words to be fulfilled and be made king of Israel. During his period of waiting, he suffered much but grew in wis-

dom and strength. Do we recognize that God is using our waiting and trials to shape, transform, and purify us into all He created us to be? (1 Sam. 16–1 Kings 2)

8. *Noah and the Ark*: Noah had to wait 120 years from God's request to build the ark until the time of the flood, enduring years of derision from others. Still, he stayed true to God's plan and was saved. He was a man of deep humility who did not look to his own understanding but stayed faithful to God's word. How do we respond when people hurt us, misunderstand us, or mistreat us? Do we pray for them and remain a witness to God's love for them, even while we are struggling? (Gen. 5–9)

9. *Moses's Time in the Desert*: Moses waited for forty years before God sent him to free the children of Israel from the Egyptians. During that time, he tended sheep because God knew that Moses was exactly the kind of careful and loving shepherd Israel needed. Moses made every excuse as to why he was not right for the job, but when God revealed himself in the burning bush, Moses learned his strength came from what God could do *through* him. Do we make excuses, or do we remain captivated by God's burning presence and allow Him to radiate love and power through us? Do we allow God to use us, even while we are on a journey to our own promised land? (Exod. 2–3)

10. *Jesus's Public Ministry*: Living a simple working-class life, Jesus had to wait thirty years to begin His ministry. Do we embrace the beauty in the ordinary and see the gift that is our own day-to-day "Nazareth life"? (Luke 3:23)

11. *Waiting for Pentecost*: The apostles had to wait ten days after Jesus's ascension before they received the Holy Spirit. God wanted them to prepare their hearts to receive this great gift. Do we allow our times of waiting to be transformative, getting our relationship with Him in perfect alignment and order? (Acts 1:1–26)

These stories show that delay does not mean denial. In each of these Biblical moments, waiting was active. God was moving and involving these people in their partnership with Him until their promises and dreams were realized.

While You're Waiting on God

As we have seen, waiting well can help us to grow in patience, perseverance, and endurance; it can also draw us closer to God. So what do we do while we wait? Here are a few suggestions:

- Believe in God's love, that He has heard you and will bring about the best thing in the perfect time. Believe that God is with you in every moment and in every step of your present situation.
- Watch with joyful expectancy for God's intervention. The answer may not be one we expect, but it will be perfect for us.
- Dive into God's Word. Scripture offers us the best opportunity to be both taught and encouraged.
- Trust in the Lord, not in your own understanding (Prov. 3:5–6). We are so tempted to depend on our own abilities rather than on God. The only way to grow in trust is to grow in relationship, and relationships take time and effort.
- Do not give in to fear or anger. If we allow ourselves to be consumed with darkness and negativity, we open a door for the enemy to take us down. St. Padre Pio tells us, "Pray, hope, and don't worry. Worry is useless. God is merciful and will hear your prayers."
- Be still. Practice patience and calmness. When we rest in God's peace, like a baby in its mother's arms, the enemy cannot bother us. When we choose to wait quietly and trustingly, we not only honor God but encourage others to put their hope in him, as well. In the quietness of our soul, God can speak to us.
- Be thankful! Speak your gratitude out loud. In Dr. Masaru Emoto's water experiment, he found the most beautiful crystals are those formed after the water is exposed to words like "love" and "gratitude." The human body is made of 70% water; our thoughts can have profound implications on our health.

- Help someone else, and take the focus off yourself. Experts say that acts of kindness boost mood, release endorphins, make us more optimistic, give us a sense of empowerment, and enrich a sense of purpose. We also tend to feel part of something greater and do not feel as lonely or isolated. A woman from my church who is elderly and has extensive health issues never focuses on what she cannot do; instead, she joyfully and creatively participates in life, and her very presence blesses and lifts others.
- Pray without ceasing. Jesus did, and He wants us to, as well. He talked with His Father in heaven often. We, too, can talk with Him anytime. And when we listen, He will share His heart with us and help us to feel safe sharing ours with Him.

The Lord is good to those who wait for Him, to the soul that seeks Him. It is good that one should wait quietly for the salvation of the Lord. (Lam. 3:25–26).

**Jesus, I trust You in the waiting.
I trust that you are listening.**

CHAPTER 5

The Mind-Body Connection

Although the world is full of suffering, is it also full of the overcoming of it.
-Helen Keller

D ressed in the thinnest of clothes in temperatures as cold as forty degrees Fahrenheit, Tibetan monks place towels soaked in cold water across the shoulders of their fellow monks, who practice a form of meditation known as *g tummo*. The combination of inadequate clothing, bitter temperatures, and wet towels is enough to induce hypothermia and eventual death in most people; however, through deep concentration, these monks are able to generate body heat. Within minutes, researchers see steam rising from the sheets; within an hour, the sheets are completely dry.[1]

Jack Schwarz, a Dutch Jewish writer who lived in a Nazi concentration camp during World War II, suffered torture beyond what most of us can comprehend. To cope, he meditated and prayed to the point of blocking out the pain and withstanding the abuse. After his release, Schwarz demonstrated his skills by putting a long sail-maker's needle through his arm. He could even regulate his blood flow, causing the puncture hole in his arm to bleed or stop bleeding at will. Researchers at the Menninger Foundation studied him and found he could indeed control many of his bodily processes with only his mind.[2]

We have heard of people suddenly exhibiting superhuman strength, like a mother lifting a car off her injured child. Scientifically, these acts cannot be attributed to adrenaline rush alone. According to Dr. Sheldon Sheps of the Mayo Clinic, "Episodes of anxiety can cause dramatic, temporary spikes in your blood pressure. If those temporary spikes occur frequently, such as every day, they can cause damage to your blood vessels, heart, and kidneys."[3] Thus, understanding how caring for our minds contributes to our physical health can help us on the path to healing.

Mind-Body Connections in Science and Scripture

Founder of the Center for Mind-Body Medicine, Dr. James Gordon says, "The brain and peripheral nervous system, the endocrine and immune systems, and indeed, all the organs of our body and all the emotional responses we have, share a common chemical language and are constantly communicating with one another." Thus, the complex relationship between our minds and bodies means that our thoughts, feelings, beliefs, and attitudes can positively or negatively affect our bodies. What we do with our physical body—what we eat, how much we exercise, the quality of our rest—can affect our mental status, and research has shown the brain has a distinct power to change the body's physiology.

In the *Mindbody Prescription,* Dr. John E. Sarno discusses what he calls the Tension Myositis Syndrome (TMS) and how the brain creates physical symptoms. The limbic system in the brain produces symptoms stemming from unconscious emotional states, such as rage, and "[w]e can influence unconscious, automatic reactions by the application of conscious thought processes. It is no longer a theory as we have seen it work in thousands of patients."[4]

Science and medicine have proven the importance of maintaining a healthy state of mind. The Bible also teaches how important the mind is to our wellbeing:

- "For God did not give us a spirit of timidity but a spirit of power and love and self-control." (2 Tim. 1:7 [RSVCE])

- "Keep your heart with all vigilance, for from it flow the springs of life." (Prov. 4:23 [RSVCE])
- "I see in my members another law at war with the law of my mind and making me captive to the law of sin which dwells in my members." (Rom. 7:23 [RSVCE])

Thus, if we watch blood-curdling horror movies or pornography, our minds become filled with images of darkness and sin, suffocating the healing process. But as Paul teaches in Philippians, "Finally, brethren, whatever is true, whatever is honorable, whatever is just, whatever is pure, whatever is lovely, whatever is gracious, if there is any excellence, if there is anything worthy of praise, think about these things" (Phil. 4:8). If we think of good and holy things, our mindset will be a fertile ground for healing.

The Mind as a Battlefield

While I was writing this book, I noticed my pain level worsened when I wrote about certain traumatic experiences. Later, I would feel relief, as if my body was unburdened of these old buried memories and no longer had to store them.

Most of us are in need of some level of healing for our memories. Traumatic experiences are part of the human condition, and each of us can recall painful memories that deeply affected us. Many years ago, my spiritual director had me recall one of these painful memories and had me place myself back in the scene. This time, however, she told me to put Jesus there with me.

In this particular memory, an elderly family member had fallen down a flight of stairs and eventually died as a result. I was the one who found her, and I blamed myself. *Why couldn't I have come home a few minutes sooner? Why did she have to lie there suffering?* I could not sleep for months because I kept replaying the scene in my mind. My anxiety skyrocketed; my physical pain increased dramatically, as well.

Then, I pictured Jesus in the scene and saw Him holding her until I got there. This strategy helped me to let go of the guilt. I was able to sleep again and replace the old tape of that memory with a new tape. If I had not dealt with my mind, I would not have been able to move on;

in healing my memories, my overall health improved.

A priest friend, who is also a widely respected trauma counselor, also taught me another valuable technique. Called EMDR (Eye Movement Desensitization and Reprocessing), this strategy alleviates distress associated with traumatic memories and helps process these memories. It helps correct negative beliefs, alleviate stress, and reduce anxiety. This tactic helped me after I witnessed a murder and could not sleep. After just fifteen minutes, the mental trauma was so drastically reduced that it no longer affected me.

In her book *Battlefield of the Mind*, Joyce Meyer writes, "The devil is a liar. Jesus called him . . . the father of lies and of all that is false (John 8:44). He lies to you and me. He tells us things about ourselves, about other people and about circumstances that are just not true. He does not, however, tell us the entire lie all at one time. He begins by bombarding our mind with a cleverly devised pattern of little nagging thoughts, suspicions, doubts, fears, wonderings, reasonings, and theories. Remember, he has a strategy for his warfare. He has studied us for a long time. He knows what we like and what we don't like. He knows our insecurities, our weaknesses and our fears. He knows what bothers us most. He is willing to invest any amount of time it takes to defeat us. One of the devil's strong points is patience."[5]

I have come to believe that our mind truly is the "battlefield." If the enemy can control us here, he can win the battle. In 2 Corinthians, Paul writes, "For though we live in the world we are not carrying on a worldly war, for the weapons of our warfare are not worldly but have divine power to destroy strongholds. We destroy arguments and every proud obstacle to the knowledge of God, and *take every thought captive* to obey Christ, being ready to punish every disobedience, when your obedience is complete" (2 Cor. 10:3–6). Satan is at war with us, trying to get us to believe God is not good. But, as Scripture tells us, "we have the divine power to destroy strongholds." We know God is good to us and gives us every help we need to win the battle.

Healing through Forgiveness

Scripture tells us, "My people are destroyed for lack of knowledge" (Hosea 4:6). In order to defeat him, we need to learn Satan's tactics and use every help and weapon God gives so that we might be restored.

Proverbs tell us, "My son, give attention to my words; incline your ear to my sayings. Do not let them depart from your sight; Keep them in the midst of your heart. For they are life to those who find them and health to all their body" (Prov. 4:20–22 [NASB]).

Our mind, and thus our health, can be affected through sin, abuse, neglect, rejection, and betrayal. All cause great emotional pain that wounds and disables us, and these wounds affect us internally and manifest physically. God, our Great Physician, can heal our broken hearts and bind our wounds, making us whole.

In Ephesians, Paul writes, "Let all bitterness and wrath and anger and clamor and slander be put away from you, along with all malice. Be kind to one another, tender-hearted, forgiving each other, just as God in Christ also has forgiven you" (Eph. 4:31–32 [NASB]). One of the first steps in the healing process is examining our hearts. We must learn the possible impediments to our healing.

Psychologists generally define forgiveness as a conscious, deliberate decision to release feelings of resentment or vengeance toward a person or group who has harmed us, regardless of whether they actually deserve forgiveness. Forgiveness does not deny the severity of the offense; it does not mean forgetting, condoning, or excusing offenses. We are not obligated to reconcile or release them from accountability. Instead, forgiveness is about us: It brings the forgiver peace of mind and frees him or her from corrosive anger. It unblocks the channel of God's healing. Jesus commands us to forgive if we are to be forgiven.

Unforgiveness is classified in medical books as a disease. According to Dr. Steven Standiford, chief of surgery at the Cancer Treatment Centers of America, refusing to forgive makes and keeps people sick. Forgiveness therapy is now being used to help treat diseases, such as cancer. He says, "It's important to treat emotional wounds or disorders because they really can hinder someone's reactions to the treatments, even someone's willingness to pursue treatment."[6]

"There is an enormous physical burden to being hurt and disappointed," says Karen Swartz, M.D., director of the Mood Disorders Adult Consultation Clinic at The Johns Hopkins Hospital. Chronic anger will result in changes to heart rate, blood pressure, and our immune response. Those changes, then, increase the risk of depression, heart disease and diabetes, among other conditions. Forgiveness, however, calms the stress response, leading to improved health.[7]

We can see the importance of forgiveness and its role in our quest for wellness. I now invite you to pray with me:

Lord Jesus, please reveal to me anyone I need to forgive. As people come to my mind, help me say, "Jesus, I forgive them."

Go back and think of those who have hurt you. Consider the circumstances, and ask God to reveal to you what may have been in their hearts when they hurt you.

Think of those people who have wounded you but refuse to acknowledge they did anything wrong . . . *Jesus, I forgive them.*

Think of someone who should have loved you and could not love you the way you needed . . . *Jesus, I forgive them.*

Think of that one person in your life who is hardest to forgive. Remember that forgiveness is a choice, not a feeling. Picture that person with you at Calvary, at the foot of the cross . . . *Jesus, I forgive them.*

Perhaps you need to forgive yourself. Failures, self-hatred, self-rejection may linger in your heart. Even if you are not accepted by others, or even yourself, Jesus always will always love you. He wants you to be free of guilt or self-condemnation . . . *Jesus, I forgive myself.*

Jesus, I forgive all these people, and I ask you to bless them with joy and with happiness. I release to you all judgment, all anger, all bitterness, all resentment. I ask you to break their power over me. In Jesus's name . . . Amen.

> *Do not be conformed to this world but be transformed*
> *by the renewal of your mind, that you may prove what is the will of God,*
> *what is good and acceptable and perfect.* (Rom. 12:2)

I trust that God is good!

CHAPTER 6

Methods of Healing

If born of God, I have power to overcome all that is not of God.
-G. V. Wigram

*N*ow Naaman, captain of the army of the king of Aram, was a great man with his master, and highly respected, because by him the Lord had given victory to Aram. The man was also a valiant warrior, but he was a leper. Now the Arameans had gone out in bands and had taken captive a little girl from the land of Israel; and she waited on Naaman's wife. She said to her mistress, "I wish that my master were with the prophet who is in Samaria! Then he would cure him of his leprosy." Naaman went in and told his master, saying, "Thus and thus spoke the girl who is from the land of Israel." Then the king of Aram said, "Go now, and I will send a letter to the king of Israel." He departed and took with him ten talents of silver and six thousand shekels of gold and ten changes of clothes. He brought the letter to the king of Israel, saying, "And now as this letter comes to you, behold, I have sent Naaman my servant to you, that you may cure him of his leprosy." When the king of Israel read the letter, he tore his clothes and said, "Am I God, to kill and to make alive, that this man is sending word to me to cure a man of his leprosy? But consider now, and see how he is seeking a quarrel against me."

It happened when Elisha the man of God heard that the king of Israel *had torn his clothes, that he sent word to the king, saying, "Why have you torn your clothes? Now let him come to me, and he shall know that there is a prophet in Israel." So Naaman came with his horses and his chariots and stood at the doorway of the house of Elisha. Elisha sent a messenger to him, saying, "Go and wash in the Jordan seven times, and your flesh will be restored to you and you will be clean." But Naaman was furious and went away and said, "Behold, I thought, 'He will surely come out to me and stand and call on the name of the Lord his God, and wave his hand over the place and cure the leper. Are not Abanah and Pharpar, the rivers of Damascus, better than all the waters of Israel? Could I not wash in them and be clean?'" So he turned and went away in a rage. Then his servants came near and spoke to him and said, "My father, had the prophet told you to do some great thing, would you not have done it? How much more then, when he says to you, 'Wash, and be clean'?" So he went down and dipped himself seven times in the Jordan, according to the word of the man of God; and his flesh was restored like the flesh of a little child and he was clean.* (2 Kings 5: 1–14)

How often do we behave like Naaman, putting God in a box and expecting him to bring about our healing in the way *we* decide is best? How often do we let God know how to do His job? Naaman has the right idea to go to God's people to get a miracle, but he becomes angry when God does not give him a miracle in the way he expects. God can use any method He chooses to bring about our healing. God's variety of methods for healing eliminates dependence on one method and shifts us from seeking our own will to trusting in His.

God's Healing through Natural Means

Sometimes, we want healing but will not do the necessary things to support it: getting quality sleep, resting, eating well, exercising, and taking medications when necessary. We must cooperate with God and let go of our opinions as to how healing should progress. We should thank God for and utilize the advances in emergency and diagnostic medicine, as well as herbs, essential oils, and non-invasive techniques and therapies that He lovingly offers us. Here are a few of the many scriptural references demonstrating God's desire for us to cooperate with the natural means He has given us:

- "When He had said this, He spat on the ground, and made clay of the spittle, and applied the clay to his eyes." (John 9:6 [NASB])
- "Now Isaiah had said, 'Let them take a cake of figs and apply it to

the boil, that he may recover.'" (Isa. 38:21 [NASB])
- "No longer drink water exclusively, but use a little wine for the sake of your stomach and your frequent ailments." (1 Tim. 5:23 [NASB])
- "By the river on its bank, on one side and on the other, will grow all kinds of trees for food. Their leaves will not wither and their fruit will not fail. They will bear every month because their water flows from the sanctuary, and their fruit will be for food and their leaves for healing." (Ezek. 47:12 [NASB])
- "[I]n the middle of its street on either side of the river was the tree of life, bearing twelve kinds of fruit, yielding its fruit every month; and the leaves of the tree were for the healing of the nations." (Rev. 22:2 [NASB])
- "And they were casting out many demons and were anointing with oil many sick people and healing them." (Mark 6:13 [NASB])

God's Healing in the Body of Christ

If we examine Scripture, we see that the most common method Jesus used to heal was the laying on of hands (twelve times), followed by commanding the person to act (eight times), then healing through the receiver's faith (seven times), speaking the Word over the person (seven times), healing through another's faith (four times), and the casting out of demons (four times). The least common method used by Jesus was rebuking the sickness (only once).

We can see also how the leaders of the early Church healed those in need:

- Invoking Jesus's name: "In the name of Jesus Christ of Nazareth rise up and walk." (Acts 3:1–8)
- Commanding the person to act: Peter only says, "Tabitha, arise, and she is raised from the dead. (Acts 9:36–43)
- Speaking the Word over them: "'Aeneas,' Peter said to him, 'Jesus Christ heals you. Get up and roll up your mat.'" (Acts 9:32–34)
- Healing through the receiver's faith: "Paul looked directly at him, saw that he had faith to be healed and called out, 'Stand up on your feet!'" (Acts 14:8–10)
- Healing through anointing: "Is anyone among you sick? Let him call for the elders of the church, and let them pray over him, anointing

him with oil in the name of the Lord. And the prayer of faith will save the one who is sick, and the Lord will raise him up." (James 5:14)

- Healing through touch and/or prayer: "Paul prayed and laid his hands on him" (Acts 28:8)

Those who have been to a healing service or received the Sacrament of the Sick may have experienced some of these methods. Other gifts of the Holy Spirit can also be present when the above methods are used. For instance, as someone is praying over another, a word of knowledge might give clues to matters of the heart that need addressing.

Also, if we have been baptized, we are called to pray with others for healing, regardless if we feel we have the particular charism of healing. God wishes us to pray for and with others but also to receive such healing prayers. Those who will not allow anyone to pray with or over them, claiming they have already prayed on their own, are limiting God and struggling for control. The Bible frequently reminds us to pray for one another: "For where two or three are gathered together in my name, there am I in the midst of them" (Matt. 18:20) or "First of all, then, I urge that supplications, prayers, intercessions, and thanksgivings be made for all people" (1 Tim. 2:1).

Scripture calls us—as the Body of Christ, as His hands and feet—to pray with others and ask for their healing and to allow others to pray with and for us. All we are required to do is pray and be available to be an instrument of God, not perform a miracle. Scripture says we are His hands and feet. In fact, St. Teresa of Avila said, "Christ has no body now but yours, no hands no feet on earth but yours." Just as He used spit and mud, He sometimes desires us to be the instrument through which He works a creative miracle. We must step out in faith and pray for others, but we also must step out in faith and allow others to pray over us, as well. Just as we go to a doctor for physical healing, we should be open to the Body of Christ for spiritual healing.

Healing through Relinquishing Control

Parents or other adults tend to form the impressions upon which we build our expectations of God. We may say that we believe in a loving God, but our images of God may be those of an abusive bully. These distorted perceptions of God impact our emotions and behaviors, as well as our ability to heal.

While most people seek physical healing, sometimes the more important and beneficial healing is emotional, spiritual, or relational; that inward work must precede any exterior manifestation. In His wisdom, God healed those very things first in my life. If I would have had the physical healing before addressing the deeper issues that broke me, I believe I would be worse off or even dead by now. The distorted and destructive self-sufficiency that brought my body to a state of complete collapse needed to be healed. Many days and nights, I cried out to God for that physical relief; in hindsight, I am able to see God's wisdom, mercy, and compassion in the way He chose to bring me out of that suffering.

When we ask for healing, there are three possible outcomes:

First, we may have an instant healing. Many people tend to believe these miracles found in the Gospels are God's standard. So many instances—the lame man who instantly rises and walks, the blind who receive their sight, the leprous men immediately healed—depict God healing in this manner. But we must remember: God's primary goal is to draw us closer to Him, and He alone knows when this type of healing would be best.

Second, our healing may be progressive. Scripture says, "They shall lay hands on the sick, and they shall *recover*" (Mark 16:18). Words in Scripture like *recover, repair,* or *restore* point to a *process*, and most healings fall into this category. A life-saving surgery will heal us, but certainly, recovery will take time.

Here is the story of the blind man at Bethsaida: "And they came to Bethsaida. And they brought a blind man to Jesus and implored Him to touch him. Taking the blind man by the hand, He brought him out of the village; and after spitting on his eyes and laying His hands on him, He asked him, 'Do you see anything?' And he looked up and said, 'I see men, for I see them like trees, walking around.' Then again He laid His hands on his eyes; and he looked intently and was restored, and began to see everything clearly" (Mark 8:22–25 [NASB]). Not every healing Jesus performed was an instant miracle. This story demonstrates a progression until full healing is achieved.

Healing may come in a few weeks' time or even in a few years. Patience, trust, and continued joyful hope must endure until His plan is perfected. When we ask God to heal us or have others pray over us for healing, God always answers in the most loving way for the greatest good. As in the case of a blind man in the Gospel of John, he was born blind "so that the works of God might be displayed in him" (John 9:1–7 [NASB]). In my case, the surgery on my SI joints was part of a study that helped further train my doctor and would eventually help many more people. My healing was progressive, and I am now blessed to be able to see how each step in the process was a loving gift rather than a cruel delay.

And sometimes, because God has a greater purpose, there is no healing at this time. This option is by far the most difficult to handle. We see in Scripture that God did not heal every problem or illness immediately. Paul had a problem with his eyesight. He also had a "thorn in his flesh, a messenger of Satan," which God did not remove. When Timothy was sick, Paul told him to drink wine but did not lay hands on him to heal him, though they were close friends. God allowed Job to suffer because He knew Job's suffering not only would end, but Job would be blessed and restored beyond what he could have dreamed. Jesus let His friend Lazarus die because He was going to transform his death into a miraculous work to glorify His Father. In the letter to Timothy, Paul says, "Erastus remained at Corinth, but Trophimus I left sick at Miletus" (2 Tim. 4:20 [NASB]). Paul could not or did not heal Trophimus; God chose a different way and time to heal him. Even the great saints of our time did not have the ability to heal whomever they wanted. All was in the control of a loving and merciful God.

C.S. Lewis wrote in his book *The Problem of Pain*, "God whispers to us in our pleasures, speaks in our conscience, but shouts in our pain: it is his megaphone to rouse a deaf world."[1] Similarly, James's letter says, "Consider it all joy, my brethren, when you encounter various trials, knowing that the testing of your faith produces endurance. And let endurance have its perfect result, so that you may be perfect and complete, lacking in nothing" (James 1:2–4 [NASB]). Thus, we do not grow in the easy times but in times of struggle. We may not understand at the time, but sometimes God desires to do so much more than give us only physical healing. Those who enter military boot camp, for example, may be undisciplined and weak; after the rigors of training, they are strong, confidant, and resilient. Often, in his infinite wisdom, God will use physical suffering to develop our character and help us grow spiritually.

St. James challenges us: "You ask and do not receive, because you ask with wrong motives, so that you may spend it on your pleasures" (James 4:3). Why do we want to be healed? What will we do when we receiving healing? Will we focus on ourselves, or will we use our healing to help others? Is our healing for the glory of God or simply for comfort's sake?

Joni Eareckson Tada's story is one of triumph and victory, despite her handicap. On July 30, 1967, Joni dove into Chesapeake Bay after misjudging the shallowness of the water. She suffered a fracture between the fourth and fifth cervical levels and became paralyzed from the shoulders down. God has used her quadriplegia and disability to help millions of people around the world. Today, Tada is an author, radio announcer, and conference speaker; she holds six doctorates and, in 1979, founded Joni and Friends, an organization to "accelerate Christian ministry in the disability community" throughout the world. In 2005, Tada was appointed to the Disability Advisory Committee of the U.S. Department of State and served on the National Council on Disability under Presidents Reagan and Bush. She is also the author of over forty-eight books on the subjects of disability and Christianity. By allowing the light of God to flow in her, Joni has done more on her healing journey than most of us will ever do, even with all of our faculties.

Hearing this story brought me awe and encouragement as I struggled; in fact, her story partially inspired me to write this book. In those many painful years, God gave and taught me so much, and I want to be a good steward of His blessings. We are not here for ourselves but to help each other reach the Kingdom. When God says, "Not now," we are being called to "arise," knowing that trusting in Him will never yield disappointment.

In our healing journeys, our challenge is to ask God what His plan is and how He would like our healing to progress. When we listen to

His heart, He will share his plan with us. Only when we allow the Holy Spirit to lead us toward that complete trust in God will we be filled with His perfect peace.

> *Afterward Jesus found him in the temple and said to him, "Behold, you have become well; do not sin anymore, so that nothing worse happens to you."*
> (John 5:14 [NASB])

**I trust that God has a perfect plan for my life
and wants the best for me.**

CHAPTER 7

Obstacles in Healing

The greater the obstacle, the more glory in overcoming it.
-Moliere

According to *Guidelines of Prayer for Healing*, published by the Doctrinal Commission of the International Catholic Charismatic Renewal Services (ICCRS), there are four basic categories of healing: physical healing from physical sickness or disability; psychological healing from wounds to the human psyche; spiritual healing that restores a person to a relationship with God; and exorcism and deliverance.[1]

In previous chapters, we have touched on a few important components of the healing process, but we must also address possible hindrances to our healing.

The Hindrance of Sin

Let's be honest: Sin is fun or else we would not want to do it. It feels good, and we get immediate gratification; it is so hard to walk away from it. God hates sin because He loves us, and He knows that sin will only hurt us and never truly make us happy. If our healing means we will keep sinning, He will not heal us. Isaiah tells us, "Your iniquities have made a separation between you and your God, and your sins have hidden His face from you so that He does not hear" (Isa. 59:2 [NASB]), and Psalm 84 says, "No good thing will He withhold from those who walk uprightly" (Ps. 84:1 [NASB]).

Healing happens when people come to repentance, a place of surrender in which God can move. Holding on to what is contrary to God's will for us removes us from Him; in patterns of sin, we cannot expect to be healed. By cooperating in any way with sin, we open the door for the enemy, so we must choose between the kingdom of darkness or the kingdom of God. Sin can actually block God's light from getting to our wounds and healing them; sin gives Satan the "legal right" to stay and harass us. The solution is simple: We must ask Jesus to reveal our soul's wounds, forgive others and ourselves, confess the sin and repent, and pray for cleansing and healing.

The Hindrance of Unforgiveness

One of the most obstructive sins is unforgiveness, which is even directly addressed in the Lord's Prayer. The Gospel of Mark says, "Whenever you stand praying, forgive, if you have anything against anyone, so that your Father who is in heaven will also forgive you your transgressions. But if you do not forgive, neither will your Father who is in heaven forgive your transgressions" (Mark 11:25 [NASB]).

As stated in Chapter 5, psychologists generally define forgiveness as a conscious decision to release feelings of resentment or vengeance toward a person or group who has harmed us, regardless of whether they actually deserve to be forgiven. Forgiveness does not mean glossing over, denying, forgetting, excusing, or condoning the offense; we are also not required to reconcile with the person or release him or her from accountability. Instead, forgiveness is about the forgiver finding peace of mind and being free from corrosive anger. (I have included in the appendix a meditation on forgiveness; I hope you find it helpful.)

The Hindrance of Fear

We fear the unknown, our weaknesses, death, pain, rejection, or the loss of control. We may even fear God, that He will take away all of the good things in our lives. But Scripture tells us that fear is not of God: "For God hath not given us the spirit of fear; but of power, and of love, and of a sound mind" (1 Tim. 1:7 [KJV]). One who fears does not trust God, and trusting God renders the devil powerless.

In my testimony, I shared that fear was a crippling part of my suffering; an already difficult situation became torturous. Yet when we are afraid, Satan has us right where he wants us. If we truly trust God, then fear has no place in and no power over us.

The Hindrance of Demonic Activity

Scripture tells us that there are demons who war against God and his people (Eph. 6:12). Unfortunately, people can accidentally open themselves up to demonic oppression, which can result in illness, depression, financial difficulty, abnormal fear, and more. Here are some ways we can open the door for a spiritual attack:

- past involvement in occult activity: Ouija boards, tarot cards, astrology, séances, necromancy, magic, psychics, divination
- New Age practices: Reiki, yoga, healing crystals, spirit guides
- past involvement in false religion: Wicca, Christian Science, Scientology
- drug use
- pornography or promiscuity
- occult meditation techniques: Emptying the mind, centering practices, or repeating one word or phrase for long periods can induce an altered state of consciousness and promote the loss of personal control of one's mind
- curses from other people or even objects: In my experience with an infected object—a sort of New Age totem pole—my pain level was next-level severe until a local exorcist came to our home to remove the demon.

The Hindrance of Refusing to Change

The Holy Spirit, or even a physician or a spouse, may ask us to make a change. For example, a doctor might ask us to change our diet, or a spouse struggling with lust might need to make changes to avoid temptation. Resisting such growth can prevent God from healing us.

The Hindrance of Pride or Self-Sufficiency

We have heard the saying, "Pride goes before the fall." Similarly, St. James tells us, "God is opposed to the proud, but gives grace to the humble" (James 4:6 [NASB]). Pride is the root of all sin because a proud person depends on himself rather than on God. Disobedience and rebellion are rooted in pride, as are mistreatment of others, failure to learn, and being a "control freak." Even being overly busy can be a manifestation of pride because we may think no one else can do our jobs as well as we.

Thus, self-sufficiency—another area of pride—can be an impediment to our healing journeys. Believing I was protecting myself from being hurt, I struggled with this sin to an unhealthy level. I was my own god and needed no one. I believed I was saving myself until God showed me the truth. Then, I began to relate to Jacob from the Old Testament, who literally wrestled with God for control. In order for Jacob to enter into his identity and future—to become "Israel"—God had to cripple his self-sufficiency.

Placing too much confidence in ourselves means we are not placing our trust in God, who alone can save us. I have known people too proud to go to a doctor or friends who have thought prayer groups beneath them. Here's a fun piece of trivia: Captain of the *Titanic* Edward Smith is noted as saying, "God Himself could not sink this ship"—pride at its finest.

The Hindrance of Instant Gratification

Heaven forbid the Wi-Fi signal causes us to have to wait a few extra seconds! Not long ago, we lived at a slower pace and had to go to a library to get information; we had more silence, more time, more patience.

Healing will sometimes require time and commitment. We may need many prayer sessions, as well as patience and a willing spirit. In "soaking prayer," prayer warriors will pray with someone until there is a breakthrough (Exo. 17:11–12, Luke 5–13). In many cases, healing may be in progress, but a lack of patience or diligence presents an obstacle as we grapple with God for control of the timing.

The Hindrance of Not Truly Desiring Healing

In some cases, a sick person enjoys being sick or does not want to put in the effort required to heal. A woman I know has been sick for years. While she attends every healing service, she gets no results; she is incredibly bitter and will not do what is asked of her, instead using her sickness to control those around her. Also, a person may be afraid of what will be required when he or she is well, so staying sick is easier—another example of the detriment of fear.

The Hindrance of Presumption

Sometimes, we are guilty of playing God and act with unwarranted confidence. We believe we know God's plan and claim our will as His. Whether we misunderstand or misinterpret God's word or create our own plan to fulfill God's promise for us, presumption means taking God's general will and saying it must happen in a certain way or time.

For example, Acts 16:31 says, "Believe in the Lord Jesus, and you will be saved, you and your household." We can inaccurately presume this means, "As long as I believe, I and my whole family will automatically be saved!" Or Psalm 91 says, "No evil shall be allowed to befall you . . . with long life I will satisfy him and show him my salvation." Presumption may tell us, "God will never let anything happen to me, and I will definitely live a long life." Even Satan told Jesus in the desert, "Look, it's in Scripture! You can jump off the temple and the angels will catch you."

In general, God wants do deliver us and bless us, but sometimes bad things happen to very good people, and holy people do not always live long lives. We know from Scripture that we *will* be delivered and blessed with Him in Heaven, but we cannot presume that each passage, especially in isolation, refers to us or the present time.

Years ago, I had a pastor friend who was much beloved by his community. When he fell ill, prayer warriors gathered to pray for healing. They all prayed, fully believing that because they came before the Lord with expectant faith, their request was already granted. Time passed; the declarations of healing and the prayers continued, but the pastor's health continued to fail. They prayed harder; they made more acts of faith. Still no results. What were they doing wrong? Did they miss something? One day, someone asked the pastor if God had given him a word about his healing. The silence was heavy: No one had asked God what his plan was. Everyone had been praying according to presumption, taking a general word from God and making it *rhema*—a word of Knowledge.

Soon after, the prayers changed. In listening to the voice of the Holy Spirit, they realized God had a different plan, and the pastor shared that God was calling him home. Instead of the frustration and confusion they had been experiencing, this prayer time became one of loving unity and joy as they helped usher him into the arms of Jesus.

Sometimes, we need to ask God how to pray, what to ask for, or to reveal Himself to us. Sometimes, we need to ask God for a specific word about our healing; if we cannot hear God, we must ask Him to help us hear His voice, and He will. We can also ask members of His Body of Christ if they have a specifical gift of discernment for us, too.

While writing this book, I fell, resulting in a near-fatal concussion. I kept repeating in the emergency room, "I will not die but live to declare the works of the Lord!" (Ps. 118:17). At home, the symptoms were still severe and frightening. I asked God for immediate healing, but I felt Him say to me, "Give me the summer, Tammy, and these symptoms will leave and never return again." No matter what I did, the symptoms persisted until the end of summer. In early September, the symptoms were dramatically reduced; by the end of the month, they were completely healed. I am still not sure why God did not instantly heal me, but with trust in Him, I could rest in His promise. I listen to the voice of my Shepherd, not trusting everything I "hear" (presumption), but taking what I hear to the body of Christ for confirmation. We must receive God's word with humility and respect, not presumption.

In the book of Daniel, three young men were about to be thrown into the fiery furnace, and they said, "Our God whom we serve is able to deliver us from the burning fiery furnace, and he will deliver us out of your hand, O king. *But if not*, be it known to you, O king, that we will not serve your gods or worship the golden image that you have set up" (Dan. 3:17–18). What they were saying was essentially, "God can do it, but even if He does not, we will be okay because we trust in Him." Their relationship with God made the outcome inconsequential.

Ultimate Healing and God's Greater Plan

Again, God does the most loving thing in the most loving way for the greatest amount of good. Sometimes, we can do all the right things and have all the faith needed, but God has a better idea to bring more hope, joy, and people to His kingdom. Life is a mystery in which we will find answers only when we meet Jesus face-to-face; God has a wonderful plan for us, even when we do not understand, and He can do the miraculous.

We have mentioned Joni Eareckson Tada, but so many other stories come to mind, as well.

Nick Vujicic is an Australian man born with the rare tetra-amelia syndrome. Despite being limbless, he became a motivational speaker with a focus on hope, life with a disability, and finding meaning. He has brought so many people to the Lord through his disability. Having addressed over three million people in over forty-four countries on five continents, he also spreads his message of hope in his book *Life Without Limits: Inspiration for a Ridiculously Good Life.*

Tony Melendez was born without any arms, yet he mastered the guitar, playing with is feet. In 1987, Melendez performed a song for Pope John Paul II and has led many young people to Christ.[2]

Fanny Crosby [3] was never healed of her blindness yet became one of the greatest Christian song writers of all time; Charlotte Elliot was a bedridden invalid when she wrote the great invitation hymn "Just As I Am," and even though she was never healed, she brought others to Christ until she died at eighty-one.[4]

We also have examples in Scripture. Paul suffered, but God did not remove the thorn in his flesh; Job suffered, but God used his suffering to defeat the devil and gave Job more blessings than he had before.

In unexplainable suffering, we must remember that God is sovereign and that He loves us more than we can imagine. When we cannot explain, when we have no conceivable answers, when our loved one passes on, or when we are not healed on this earth—these sufferings gauge the depth of our relationship with God.

In John 11, we see how Martha responded to such a test in her relationship with Christ:

When Martha heard that Jesus was coming, she went and met him, while Mary sat in the house. Martha said to Jesus, "Lord, if you had been here, my brother would not have died. And even now I know that whatever you ask from God, God will give you." Jesus said to her, "Your brother will rise again." Martha said to him, "I know that he will rise again in the resurrection at the last day." Jesus said to her, "I am the resurrection and the life; he who believes in me, though he dies, yet shall he live, and whoever lives and believes in me shall never die. Do you believe this?" She said to him, "Yes, Lord; I believe that you are the Christ, the Son of God, he who is coming into the world." (John 11:20–27)

Jesus ignored Martha's plea to help her brother before he died, yet Martha responds with faith, trusting Him although she does not understand.

So many Christians' illnesses, disabilities, and deaths have been witnesses to the world because they knew profound suffering but still trusted God. They were living witnesses to the joy of the Lord, and no circumstance could take that joy away from them.

Misunderstandings about Sickness

Many have been told that sickness equates to carrying our cross after Jesus; thus, we must embrace sickness because it is a blessing from God. Our cross does not simply mean sickness; for example, we may endure ridicule from friends and family when we convert to Christianity. God can use sickness and bring good out of it; however, sickness is an evil, and God is not the author of any evil.

Only a *few* chosen souls have been specifically called by God and have joyfully offered themselves to be victim souls in a vocation known as "redemptive sufferers." However, this vocation is not God's will for every sick person.

When I was bedridden and suffering, well-meaning friends told me to bear my torture joyfully because God was giving me this special gift. This belief can be damaging to a person's relationship with God because he or she might then view God as untrustworthy or someone to fear. Just as parents would not want to watch their child suffer with cancer, God loves us deeply and wants good things for us.

When God calls people to the *vocation* of redemptive suffering,

He will ask them, and they will gladly *want* it. They will be filled with joy and peace and the desire to be united with Jesus in this way. Thus, you are likely not called to this vocation, so cooperate with God on your journey to wholeness. Plus, Jesus did not stay on the cross; He rose! Our suffering is temporary, and wonderful things await when it passes.

Sharing with Christ

Sickness is an evil that sometimes God allows. I am so glad I did not accept my own torturous suffering as "God's will" and stay in that dark place where I could not see a loving God. Instead, I moved to a place of trying to know Him—who He was and what He wanted from me. I could then see my suffering as a gift; without it, I would have never uncovered the deeper sins and blocks from which God was trying to free me, working through the inner healing that God wanted for me.

Isaiah says, "Behold, I have refined you, but not as silver; I have tried you in the furnace of affliction" (Isa. 48:10). Sin douses His radiant light in us. My period of suffering was a time to walk in such a refining fire so that the dross of sin could be burned away and reveal the precious gold He placed deep within me.

When we are suffering, we should unite our pain to Jesus's sufferings on the Cross for the good of others: "Now I rejoice in my sufferings for your sake, and in my flesh I complete what is lacking in Christ's afflictions for the sake of his body, that is, the church" (Col. 1:24). We are a royal priesthood and graced to share in Christ's work of saving souls. Just like priests, who offer sacrifice, we are invited to share in God's redemptive work.

There are countless stories of people who have participated in such suffering for a higher purpose.

A Christian mother prayed for years, asking God to save her atheist son, but she saw little change. One day, she prayed, "Anything, God! I will do anything, suffer anything, just as long as you save my son!" Soon after, she was diagnosed with stomach cancer. Through her suffering, her son drew closer to his mother and became a committed Christian who has given his life to lead others to Christ, as well; she was rewarded and overjoyed at seeing her son's transformation. Despite her pain, she was joyous because, not only were her prayers answered, but she was being allowed to participate in the plan of her son's salvation.

In 1942 in the Netherlands, a stranger knocked on a door and handed an eight-year-old girl to the safekeeping of an unknown neighbor. The Jewish girl, Lien de Jong[5], would never see her parents again, but her parents had made the agonizing decision to save her from the Nazis by losing her. Their suffering lasted a lifetime, but it was worth the price of saving their daughter's life.

Andrew Leitch was shopping with his elderly parents and baby in Sydney when a car smashed into the storefront at forty-five miles per hour—straight toward the Leitches. Andrew positioned himself to take the full impact, scooping his son out of the way. Leitch's legs were crushed, but he held on, thinking, "I can take the hit . . . I can repair, but there's no way my son is going to repair."[6]

A teenaged mother finds herself pregnant by extraordinary means, and her fiancé does not understand and wants to divorce her. She perseveres and, near delivery, rides a donkey through rugged terrain to eventually give birth in a stable. Bethlehem means "house of bread," and a manger was a feeding trough. Jesus would be the Living Bread from Heaven. Mary's "yes" at the Annunciation did not mean "Yes, I want to have a baby and live happily ever after" but, instead, that she would stand in the crowd to watch her Son be humiliated and crucified.

I would bet that, if we asked any of these people if they would trade their pain and give up the fruits of their sacrifice, none of them would.

If Satan knew Jesus would use all of His suffering to save us, perhaps he would not have tortured Jesus like he did. Each lash, each thorn, each slap was Jesus making up for our sin to give us His Father's inheritance. Satan cannot understand suffering because he cannot understand love. He believed Jesus's suffering would make Jesus curse His father. Satan could not understand a love so great that it would accept pain for someone else's sake. As with all of these examples, true love does not count the cost.

In our humanity, we can do nothing; when we are united to Jesus, He makes our actions divine. He takes our "loaves and fishes" and works miracles for the good of the Kingdom (John 6:9–13). A parent baking a cake with a small child loves to share that experience, and the child is so happy to contribute, even if he is just handing his parent a spoon; when they together present the cake, made with love, to the family, joy radiates from their faces.

Jesus asks us to imitate Himself in everything, and because he loves us so much, He takes our tiny offering into the furnace of His divine love and brings forth something much greater than our frail human act. We are told, "For to this you have been called, because Christ also suffered for you, leaving you an example, so that you might follow in his steps" (1 Pet. 2:21). Thus, now is an excellent time to examine our lives and correct anything that does not align with God's plan for our holiness.

Sickness vs. Suffering

Sickness is defined as 1) "impairment of normal physiological function affecting part or all of an organism" and 2) "a disease or malady." Sickness is an evil; God is not the author of sickness.

To suffer means to undergo pain, distress, or loss. Being human, all of us will experience moments of suffering or pain until we get to Heaven; God never promises a life devoid of suffering, but Jesus said, "These things I have spoken to you, that in Me you may have peace. In the world you will have tribulation; but be of good cheer, I have overcome the world" (John 16:33).

Pain can be good; it can alert us that something is wrong or needs repairing or removal. Pain and suffering can move us to a place of change and growth, and God can use them to help bring us to a higher good. Once change comes about, pain and suffering no longer serve their intended purposes and should dissipate. Thus, finding the *source* of suffering, bringing it to light, and healing it will bring long-term healing. If I place my finger over a flame, my body will react with pain. This pain is good because it tells me that my body is in danger. However, no matter how many prayers I say, the pain will not be alleviated until I move my finger away from the source.

Suffering is also rooted in mental and spiritual pain. When God helped me deal with the fear in my life, my suffering was considerably reduced. Anyone who is sick wants healing, of course, but also for the suffering to end. I knew a person who struggled with temptations of suicide who would say, "I don't really want to kill myself. I just want the suffering to stop." All suffering is temporary and will end, and thus we must trust that God, who loves us more than we can understand, will help us through until the suffering ceases. We are not helpless but, rather, can ask God to show us the way through . . . and He will!

When Jesus spoke of suffering, He referred to obstacles and hardships mostly concerning our Christian walk. When sickness is mentioned, healing is almost always promised. We can have hardships, pain, and struggle but still be filled with hope, peace, and joy; when we need healing, we can also be filled with hope and peace because we can trust in a God who loves us deeply. We do not know the mind of God to understand why suffering exists, just like a child about to undergo a life-saving surgery may not understand but trusts his parents know best. Jesus tells us we must be like children: "Truly I say to you, unless you are converted and become like children, you will not enter the kingdom of Heaven" (Matt. 18:3).

Heaven belongs to children because of their purity of heart and innocent and trusting natures. Jesus wants us to become like children. A small child trusts his parents and does not blame, turn away, or become suspicious of them, yet we do so to God our Father. No wonder we do not experience the kingdom of Heaven on earth.

We might not be perfectly restored physically in this life, but suffering must not dominate our lives. So much of our suffering originates in our minds and attitudes, but we do not need to be weighed down by it or give it power. Instead, we can choose to radiate joy and live a good life.

Let each of you look not only to his own interests,
but also to the interests of others. (Phil. 2:4)

I trust God enough to give up my plans and presumptions.
I trust Him enough to give Him my crutches.
I trust that He wants my suffering to end.

CHAPTER 8

Other Tools in the Toolbox

When we are powerless to do a thing, it is a great joy that we can come and step inside the ability of Jesus.
-Corrie Ten Boom

A s Scripture tells us, we are more than conquerors. We are not helpless! We have addressed some hindrances to healing and are now ready to explore some other useful tools and strategies.

Knowing Your Authority

In the company Perdue Farms, known for its chicken production, the son, Frank, acted and administered on behalf of his father, Arthur. He did not sheepishly direct; he knew his identity. He spoke and led with confidence, not by his own authority but by that which his father exercised through him. Frank inherited all that his father had, and he now passes on that same authority to his own son.

We are sons and daughters of the King; if we are in His Will, we walk in His authority and can exercise it to further God's plan. Jesus has "given [us] authority to tread on serpents and scorpions, and over all the power of the enemy" (Luke 10:19). If the enemy has laid opposition, we can walk in our God-given authority and trample over his deceptions and schemes. Thus, if we see something that stands in the way of God's will in our lives, we bear the responsibility to overcome that obstacle. God has given us the tools and the authority in Christ.

Many people falsely believe the enemy has great power and that we should fear it. But we must remember that *Satan has no power unless God permits it*. And why would God allow it? One principal reason is because He will not interfere with our free will. We bear the responsibility to distance ourselves from the enemy. Generally speaking, Satan can attack or harass us only if we give him the invitation to do so, either through cooperating in sin or giving him an entrance through fear. A guard dog on a leash has dominion over only a certain area, so the dog can hurt us only if we enter his territory. He can also smell fear, giving him the impetus to attack. Jesus has chained Satan and given you the authority as His representative on earth to walk in freedom. We are sons and daughters of the King (1 John 3:1), we are His heir and possess what He possesses (Luke 15:31), and we are made in God's image and have dominion (Gen. 1:26–28).

In the Gospel of Luke, we hear more about this authority: "When Jesus had called the Twelve together, he gave them power and authority to drive out all demons and to cure disease. And He sent them out to proclaim the kingdom of God and to perform healing" (Luke 9:1). The Scripture makes clear that God has given authority to His Church to cast out demons and to heal diseases; the purpose of this authority is that we use it to proclaim the kingdom of God. God, not the powers of darkness, is supreme. Jesus gave the apostles authority to proclaim God's kingdom and to set the people free from the kingdom of Satan; we are called to do the same.

God is the source of all authority and gives it to us to maintain His order (1 Cor. 14:33, 40). Thankfully, we are under God's authority, so to exercise it means to carry out what He wants: love, light, peace, joy, freedom, victory, wholeness, salvation. Anything that works against these things must be cast out and overcome. By His Word, we cast out fear and take authority over the spirit of despair. We can bind any spirit of sickness or oppression in the Name of Jesus and by His precious Body and Blood. We can declare His will and give no place to the enemies' lies.

St. Peter says, "You are a royal priesthood, a chosen race. You are

God's own possession" (1 Pet. 2:9), and we bear responsibility to live this out (CCC 783). As we embrace our identity and walk in His authority, we begin to do things we never thought possible. We grow, succeed, and blossom.

We are told we must walk in this authority, but we are not told that we are responsible for the outcome. We must step out in faith and leave the rest to God. Great miracles are being done in third-world countries because they know, accept, and live out who they are in Christ and have complete confidence in what Jesus has given to them.

We are to be the hands and feet of Christ in this world. This task is not up to someone else, so we must allow Christ to live so completely in us that we dissolve in the sea of His divine will. He will then speak and work through us. His authority, power, and light will break Satan's strongholds and send the powers of darkness scurrying like frightened cockroaches!

Declarations

Proverbs 18 tells us, "Death and life are in the power of the tongue" (Prov. 18:21). Authority is exercised through our spoken word, so we can use, speak, and proclaim God's powerful word.

What we speak has consequences: We can bring negativity and darkness, or we can use what we speak to strengthen our faith, be a weapon in spiritual warfare, make us ready for God's movement in our lives, and lift our spirits. We can be a light for others, too.

We must speak also these declarations out loud: Not only are we affected by hearing the words, but they can also change the spiritual atmosphere, causing the enemy to flee. There are many wonderful resources about declarations and decrees, but simply speaking favorite Scripture passages works, as well. We may declare verses such as "I can do all things through Christ who strengthens me" (Phil. 4:13), "God blesses me and surrounds me with favor as a shield" (Ps. 5:12), or "God has not given me a spirit of fear. He gives me power, love, and a sound mind" (2 Tim. 1:7). Commit them to memory, so they can be utilized at a moment's notice.

Jesus tells us, "If you abide in Me, *and My words abide in you*, ask whatever you wish, and it will be done for you" (John 15:7 [NASB]). We also know that "the *word* of God is living and active and sharper than any two-edged sword" (Heb. 4:12). Thus, we *must* have God's Word, which is foundational to healing, in our mouths at all times. Abide in God's intimate, trusting relationship, and speak and declare His word.

Praise

I read *Prison to Praise* by Merlin Carothers[1] early in my journey. I learned that when we praise God, no matter what else is going on, we break Satan's hold. If the devil is trying to defeat us or turn us away from God, praising God in the midst of or even *for* the enemy's attack will strike a fatal blow to Satan. While he tries to use pain and suffering to turn us against God, if we turn even more toward God because of the suffering, he will not want to use that tactic anymore.

Sacraments

Catholics have some of the greatest healing tools: the sacraments. The Catechism states, "The Church believes in the life-giving presence of Christ, the physician of souls and bodies. This presence is particularly active through the sacraments, and in an altogether special way through the Eucharist, the bread that gives eternal life and that St. Paul suggests is connected with bodily health" (CCC 1509).

The Church prays for the sick at every Mass—the most powerful of all prayers because it is the offering of the sacrifice of Jesus to the Father. During Mass, we take Jesus—Body, Blood, Soul, and Divinity—physically into our bodies and become one with Him. Despite its power, so few avail themselves of this grace because they are either unaware or have little faith. Yet St. Paul reminds us, "For he who eats and drinks, eats and drinks judgment to himself if he does not judge the body rightly. For this reason many among you are weak and sick" (1 Cor. 11:29–30).

We also have the Sacrament of Reconciliation in which we confess our sins to God, repent, and resolve to walk away from those sins. James 5:16 says, "Therefore, confess your sins to one another, and pray for one another so that you may be healed." There is power and healing in this sacrament! It has become one of my favorites because of the freedom I experience each time I go. Reconciliation offers a great opportunity to unburden our hearts and receive the strength to start fresh again. Many exorcists say that this sacrament is more powerful than exorcism in freeing people from Satan's stronghold.

The Church provides another channel of healing: Anointing of the Sick. When we receive this sacrament, which helps unite those who suffer with Jesus's saving and healing power, we receive healing on some level. We receive forgiveness of our sins, comfort in our suffering, restoration of our spirit, and sometimes even the return of physical health. As James 5:14–15 describes, hands are laid on the sick, who are anointed with blessed oil. The Anointing of the Sick conveys several graces and imparts the Holy Spirit's gifts of strengthening against anxiety, discouragement, and temptation, and it conveys peace and fortitude (CCC 1520).

Prayers of Saints

Another angel came and stood at the altar, holding a golden censer; and much incense was given to him, so that he might add it to the prayers of all the saints on the golden altar which was before the throne. (Rev. 8:3 [NASB])

Catholics believe that the prayers of the saints in heaven, who are freed from earthly limitations and are now in the very presence of God, are very powerful. We do not pray *to* the saints, but we ask for their intercession, much as we might ask as a family member to pray for us. James says, "The effective prayer of a righteous man can accomplish much" (James 5:16 [NASB]). We are all one body and one family; death does not diminish that. How blessed are we as Christians that we believe in the communion of saints!

Paul says, "For just as we have many members in one body and all the members do not have the same function, so we, who are many, are one body in Christ, and individually members one of another" (Rom. 12:4–5 [NASB]). He also tells us, "God has so composed the body, giving more abundant honor to that member which lacked, so that there may be no division in the body, but that the members may have the same care for one another. And if one member suffers, all the members suffer with it; if one member is honored, all the members rejoice with it" (1 Cor. 12:24–27 [NASB]). Thus, as members of the Body of Christ—both in Heaven and on earth—we are called to pray with and for each other; all intercessions matter.

Through the Church's history, many documented and proven healings and miracles have been connected with holy places (Lourdes, France, for instance), as well as from the presence of the relics of certain saints. In Acts 19:12, the sick had only to touch Paul's handkerchief or be in his shadow to be healed. Canonization of a saint requires at least two documented and authenticated miracles; eyewitnesses alone are considered insufficient. Medical, scientific, psychiatric, and theological experts are consulted; only evidence that is immediate, spontaneous, and inexplicable is considered. Our brothers and sisters in Christ that have gone before us are living what we are yearning for here on earth. They are living fully in God's kingdom, and they can and want to help us.

Angels

Angels are pure spirits created by God. *Angel* comes from the Greek *angelos*, meaning "messenger." In the Bible, "angel" nearly always applies to heavenly beings.

All of us have guardian angels. From conception until death, human life is surrounded by their watchful care and intercession. The Catechism states, "'Beside each believer stands an angel as protector and shepherd leading him to life.' Already here on earth the Christian life shares by faith in the blessed company of angels and men united in God" (CCC 336). Jesus says, "Take heed that ye despise not one of these little ones; for I say unto you, That in heaven their angels do always behold the face of my Father which is in heaven" (Matt. 18:10 [KJV]).

Raphael, which mean "Healing Power of God," is an angel mentioned in Scripture who played a pivotal role in the Book of Tobit (a book from the Septuagint Biblical canon) as he helped Tobit's son Tobias on his journey. Traditionally, due to the meaning of his name, Raphael is revered as the Archangel of Healing; thus, he might be alluded to in John:

> Now there is in Jerusalem by the sheep gate a pool, which is called in Hebrew Bethesda, having five porticoes. In these lay a multitude of those who were sick, blind, lame, and withered, waiting for the moving of the waters; for an angel of the Lord went down at certain seasons into the pool and stirred up the water; whoever then first, after the stirring

up of the water, stepped in was made well from whatever disease with which he was afflicted. (John 5:2–4 [NASB])

Our guardian angels love us and will do everything within God's Will to protect us from harm, although we sometimes step out of God's protection when we sin and do not repent. Our guardian angels, along with the archangels and other angels, also intercede for us in prayer. (See Tob. 12:12, Rev. 5:8, and Rev. 8:3.)

Therapies

I highly recommend researching complimentary therapies as you work with your doctor on a physical issue. As a medical professional, I can tell you from experience that most doctors are not generally trained in a variety of modalities such as nutrition, facial release, craniosacral therapy, and more. I highly recommend integrative health care that brings conventional and complementary approaches together in a coordinated way. It emphasizes a patient-focused approach to health care and wellness; it usually includes mental, emotional, functional, spiritual, and social elements—treating the whole person rather than one specific issue. A few of these additional therapies to be considered might be biofeedback, craniosacral therapy, massage therapy, hydrotherapy, essential oils, nutrition, herbal therapies, and chiropractic or osteopathic treatments.

My suggestion is to not just accept illness or pain as part of life without first researching all available options. Pray, but also work with what is provided in the natural realm. Recently, a friend of mine was suffering with what appeared to be severe arthritis; we prayed, but nothing improved. After running multiple tests and trying different arthritis medications without success, his doctor decided to check his vitamin D level and discovered it was extremely low. Once this supplementation was initiated, the relief was practically immediate. The arthritic symptoms disappeared. I believe our prayers helped too because the doctor was able to target the root of the problem and correct it.

My multiple surgeries—which involved cutting through core muscles, adhesions, and scarring—created many problems. My doctors did not know how to address these issues except through medication; as most people in this situation discover, medication alone is often ineffective. Through a technique called facial release, my physical therapist was able to undo some of the tissue restrictions, thereby significantly reducing post-surgical pain. My only word of caution is to seek out only those complementary therapies that are in line with our Christian faith and avoid any New Age options.

Other Suggestions

- Have an expectant faith: "And the Lord said, 'If you had faith like a mustard seed, you would say to this mulberry tree, "Be uprooted and be planted in the sea"; and it would obey you'" (Luke 17:6 [NASB]). Have faith that the Lord can work in and through you for His glory.
- Take advantage of prayer teams if you are able, or join a prayer group for support.
- Make time to pray and sit with God. Soak in His presence. If you are Catholic, go to an adoration chapel and bask in His physical presence.
- Read uplifting books about others who have been healed or inspiring stories of those who have overcome great hardships, knowing you are not alone in your struggle.
- Laugh! Laughter is incredibly healing, and God so loves to see you smile.

Because you have made the Lord your refuge, the Most High your habitation, no evil shall befall you, no scourge come near your tent. For he will give his angels charge of you to guard you in all your ways. On their hands they will bear you up, lest you dash your foot against a stone. (Ps. 91:9–12)

I trust that God wants me to be really, truly happy.
I trust that God my Father wants to see me smile.

CHAPTER 9

Spiritual Warfare

A man who leans on God is immovable and cannot be overthrown.
-St. Claude de la Colombiere

S t. Peter tells us, "Be sober, be vigilant; because your adversary the devil, as a roaring lion, walketh about, seeking whom he may devour" (1 Pet. 5:8 [KJV]). Many of Satan's victims do not even know a war is going on, so they are easy prey. As Christians, we know we are in the midst of a great spiritual battle and that we must be prepared, so we may have the victory. If we know a hurricane is coming, we take necessary precautions; so much more should we be vigilant against the attacks of the evil one.

Then, there are those who acknowledge the battle but do not understand the nature of Satan's plans and weapons or the weapons that God has provided for our defense. St. Paul tells us, "Finally, be strong in the Lord and in the strength of his might. Put on the whole armor of God, that you may be able to stand against the wiles of the devil. For we are not contending against flesh and blood, but against the principalities, against the powers, against the world rulers of this present darkness, against the spiritual hosts of wickedness in the heavenly places" (Eph. 6:10–12 [RSVCE]).

Many people suffer needlessly because, when suffering is caused by Satan's attack, deliverance is available. His strongholds can be broken, and healing can be a reality. He does not want you to have any good thing that God has planned for your life; he wants to destroy and steal every blessing from you (Jn. 10:10).

Healing can be sought not only in the physical realm but in the spiritual realm, too. God desires us to be whole and protected. He is our loving Father and, as any good Father, He wants us to live our lives abundantly (Jn. 10:10). As Christians, we must realize who we are in Christ: We belong to another kingdom, the kingdom of God, and we have God's promise that He will defend us and help us to overcome the enemy.

For healing and deliverance, as most Christians agree, we must first confess our sins. We cannot have any agreement with the enemy, or he will not leave us alone. Then, we must repent, renounce the sin, believe that Jesus can free us, take authority over the enemy, cast him out, and ask the Holy Spirit to fill us. We must not forget to constantly give God praise: The enemy hates this, and will flee.

I have studied under our diocese's exorcist and was part of a deliverance ministry, so I would like to offer a brief word of caution. Satan is very legalistic, so we cannot blindly go up against him unless we know some basic rules. We have authority over ourselves, our spouses, and our children. We have authority over all that pertains to us: our homes, health, vehicles, friendships, ministry, finances, etc. We cannot use "authority" over a demon that is not under our natural authority; we will only antagonize it. But always remember that God is sovereign, and we are His children. When we realize who we are in Christ, the enemy can never have any power over us.

The enemy has as much power as God allows. He can do nothing without getting permission from God first. God will allow Satan's attacks only if they will help us turn from sin and grow in holiness.

Remember: If Satan can draw us away from God and into sin, he will have the legal right to attack us. Here are some of Satan's tactics[1]:

- *Breaking our will to fight.* The devil's plot is to harass us until we lose our will to fight and give up. He will not stop until one of two things happen: He breaks our will to fight back, or we take the Sword of the Spirit and make him flee.

- *Wearing us down.* If Satan can wear us down mentally and exhaust us physically, he has an easy time controlling us. He will try to get us worried about the economy, war, finances, family issues, or anything to take us away from the peace of God. He will keep us overly busy, even with good spiritual things to drain our strength and resources. Once we are spiritually incapacitated, he can have his way.

- *Simultaneously attacking on all fronts*—including our jobs, physical health, emotional health, marriages, families, ministries, and businesses. Sometimes, this tactic is a clue to who is behind our infirmity. If we find ourselves under attack from multiple points at the same time, we must remember Satan is behind it and run to Jesus.

- *Dividing and conquering.* Satan uses this weapon to destroy marriages, families, ministries, friendships, businesses, and any type of good relationship or partnership. If he creates division, arguments, misunderstandings, or hurt, destruction ensues. We must remain aware and counter these attacks with understanding and love.

- *Scaring us.* If Satan can get us into fear, we are done. We must know God's power, the enemy's strategies, and who we are in Christ. Keep in mind that Satan cannot do *anything* on his own. Even to tempt or harass us, he must have God's permission. He is a chained junkyard dog: He can scare us but has no power to hurt us unless we get too close to him.

- *Rushing and crushing.* Charles Stanley once talked about this strategy of the enemy. He used the acronym HALT: Hungry, Angry/Agitated, Lonely, Tired. If the enemy can weaken us in these ways, he will rush in to crush us. We must be aware of these typical weak spots and prevent them. Also, when we give place to the enemy by living in sin—whether by omission or commission—we have exposed ourselves to the devil; in most cases, he will take this opportunity, as well, to rush in and crush us.

- *Finding our weakness and exploiting it.* An easy way to victory is to attack the weak. The kingdom of darkness is always looking for weak areas in our spiritual lives. When a weakness is revealed, Satan will attack it ferociously, so we must be strong in the Lord. Here are some common inroads:

- *Cravings and passions.* He will try to get us addicted to foods, beverages, alcohol, or drugs. The same holds for passions: The enemy will try to get us out of balance and make a god out of anything we have affection for or devotion to.
- *Sexuality.* God meant sexual expression to be a great gift when used as designed. The enemy will take this beautiful and powerful good and try to destroy us with it.
- *Media.* Music, TV, movies, social media—What we take in to our minds never leaves. Every pornographic or violent image stays in our memories. Music can be especially dangerous. Scripture tells us that Satan was the worship leader of heaven and earth (Ezek. 28:11–19), so he understands its power (Dan. 3:1–7).
- *Wounds.* If a wound—physical, emotional, or spiritual—is left untreated, it festers, gets infected, and can kill.
- *Sin.* By cooperating with our sin or someone else's, we give Satan an inroad to abuse us.
- *Loneliness.* If he can get us alone, we are weak prey. A YouTube video showed an antelope straying from its herd, making it prey to lions. When the rest of the herd saw, they surrounded the weak stray and warded off the attack. Those who say they do not need church or community because they pray to God on their own are putting themselves in unnecessary danger.
- *Self-debasement.* When we do not know our identity and value in Christ, we are easy prey to the enemy's lies.

We must review these tactics often, being aware so we do not give Satan an inroad to hurt us. He can inflict sickness on us if we give him the chance. If we are in any way in agreement with the kingdom of darkness—if we open the door even a crack to let Satan get a foothold—he has the legal right to attack us. We must confess and renounce sin, asking God for forgiveness and the Holy Spirit to fill us with the gifts needed to counter sin.

Satan is a liar and a counterfeiter; he tempts us into thinking that what he offers will make us happy and satisfied. "Eat the entire gallon of ice cream," he will tell us. "It will make you feel so good. God just wants to deprive you." Later, we end up physically ill and disgusted with ourselves. Satan hates us so much. Why give him the satisfaction of seeing us defeated and miserable?

We are overcomers. We are victors. In order to walk in victory, we must first face Goliath. Only by standing strong through the battle can we achieve victory.

The Last Attack

As I was preparing to write these last chapters, our country and our world was in a state of emergency due to the coronavirus. I was isolated, alone, and in pain; I was not able to get to any of the therapies that were helping me along the final stretch of my healing journey, and I was under full attack from the enemy. Satan was trying to get me into fear. I was sick, and every time I would recover for a day or so, within twenty-four hours, something else would come upon me.

At first, I wondered why God was allowing the enemy to come against me, but I began to feel that God was going to use the experience to strike him with a crushing blow: "That with which he attacks shall become his own poison."

I remembered all that I had learned, and I went through this book, utilizing each tool. I looked at my sin to see if I had any open doors to give the enemy a foothold. I took authority over what I could, but nothing seemed to work. One day, I was so sick and could not write; within minutes of getting up, I would have to head back to bed. I asked Jesus why I was suffering.

He showed me a battle scene in which blood-stained hatchets were thrown at me as I was surrounded on three sides by darkness. Jesus stood behind me, telling me to direct those weapons back to my assailants. I thought about Heaven—a place of perfect peace and joy as saints and angels direct all of their attention, all of their praise, to God. I began to praise God, thanking Him in the midst of this storm. Even in the obscurity, I could thank Him because I was confident the light was going to break through. I praised and praised, using Scripture verses and whatever else the Holy Spirit put on my heart. I told Him how much I trusted Him, and I *felt* it.

A deep peace and joy slowly filled my soul. The enemy was in a rage. The hatchets were falling to the ground before they could harm me. Instead of feeling weak and helpless like the enemy wanted, I felt the power of the Almighty God flowing through me. Jesus allowed me to feel His presence so strongly that I knew He was with me, that I was not alone.

Then, the breakthrough—the spiritual realm broke open. I was on the battlefield, and all was silent, just Jesus and me. The finish line was now in sight. He made me aware that the battle was *His* to fight, not mine. All I had to do was trust and praise Him, knowing my Daddy God was right here. I could trust Him on this level because a solid relationship was already in place.

Psalm 144 says, "Blessed be the Lord, my rock, who trains my hands for war, and my fingers for battle; he is my steadfast love and my fortress, my stronghold and my deliverer, my shield and he in whom I take refuge, who subdues peoples under me" (Ps. 144:1–2 [ESV]). I heard the throngs of victory shouts in the distance. What the enemy had meant for my destruction God meant for my victory (Gen. 50:20).

An analytical soul, I wanted to know what those hatchets represented. Indeed, God was showing me the last piece of the puzzle to usher me to victory. Though the answer did not come immediately—I prayed for over a month before He clearly showed me—I was surprised to learn the hatchets were *lies*. I had been believing many lies and had not been receiving the truth.

As I prayed, I began to see the areas where I accepted these lies: believing God wanted me to suffer, that I would be special only if I were a "suffering servant," that my body could not heal, that I was constantly in danger. I believed the lie that I had to be afraid, that I had to be the savior and fixer of all of the wrongs in my life. Since childhood, I was never allowed to be a little girl but had to be strong and take care of everyone else, even in unreasonable and ridiculous situations. For instance, at eight years old, I believed I had to protect everyone from the neighborhood bully. Or when I was in labor for my first child, I was fixing the plumbing in my basement at 2:00 A.M. because my husband had a meltdown and "could not handle it" (the thought never occurred to me call a plumber!). I finally saw these false beliefs for what they were: lies.

I began to reject each lie out loud and replace it with God's truth. God loved me. I was safe. I was His princess. Accepting these truths was the key that unlocked me from my prison of pain where I could not see these realities through the mire of lies that clogged my mind and spirit.

God permits attacks for many reasons, most often to strengthen and raise us to a new spiritual level. If we are in relationship with Him, even disasters will not shake us because our eyes are always trustingly fixed on our God. He is not the author of sickness or tragedies; He never wills them but will use them if they can bring us higher.

Through the Covid-19 pandemic, a war that Satan is waging and that God is temporarily allowing, God intends to bring a greater good. Many are re-evaluating their priorities, rediscovering simpler home and family lives. Eyes and hearts are receiving light; evil is being exposed and finally brought to justice. Financial institutions are being reworked. In fact, this book came to be as a result of the lockdown.

God has been actively working to usher in a new normal—not the doom and gloom the media offers but a new freedom and way of life that will be so much better than before the pandemic. When we cannot make sense of a situation or fathom the big picture, all we need to do is trust in the One who does.

Satan is the ruler of *this* world but only for a time. Jesus came that we may have life abundantly. I believe that Satan's time is coming to an end—thus his unrelenting persecution of so many of God's children—and that he is going to be chained for a long while. Many saints and prophets have spoken about this new era, and Scripture itself reveals it to us, as well: "Then I saw an angel come down from heaven, holding in his hand the key to the abyss and a heavy chain. He seized the dragon, the ancient serpent, which is the Devil or Satan, and tied it up for a thousand years and threw it into the abyss, which he locked over it and sealed, so that it could no longer lead the nations astray until the thousand years are completed. After this, it is to be released for a short time" (Rev. 20:1–3).

Isaiah also shares a similar idea:

"For behold, I create new heavens and a new earth; and the former things will not be remembered or come to mind but be glad and rejoice forever in what I create; for behold, I create Jerusalem for rejoicing and her people for gladness. I will also rejoice in Jerusalem and be glad in My people; and there will no longer be heard in her the voice of weeping and the sound of crying. No longer will there be in it an infant who lives but a few days, or an old man who does not live out his days; for the youth will die at the age of one hundred and the one who does not reach the age of one hundred will be thought accursed. They will build houses and inhabit them; they will also plant vineyards and eat their fruit. They will not build and another inhabit, they will not plant and another eat; for as the lifetime of a tree, so will be the days of My people, and My chosen ones will wear out the work of their hands. They will not labor in vain, or bear children for calamity; for they are the offspring of those blessed by the Lord, and their descendants with them. It will also come to pass that before they call, I will answer; and while they are still speaking, I will hear. The wolf and the lamb will graze together, and the lion will eat straw like the ox; and dust will be the serpent's food. They will do no evil or harm in all My holy mountain," says the Lord. (Isa. 65:17–25 [NASB])

In a report from Vatican City on February 14, 2001, Pope John Paul II discussed this new era, as well:

In the new era brought by Christ, the Pope explained, "God and man, man and woman, humanity and nature are in harmony, in dialogue, in communion. The authentic new era is nothing other than the reestablishment of the lost relation between God and man. Christ must cancel the work of devastation, the horrible idolatry, violence and every sin that the rebellious Adam has spread in the secular affairs of humanity and on the horizon of creation. He recapitulates Adam in himself, in whom the whole of humanity recognizes itself; he transfigures him into son of God, he brings him to full communion with the Father," the Pope explained. Christ's new era also embraces "nature itself . . . subjected as it is to lack of meaning, degradation, and devastation caused by sin," which will thus participate "in the joy of the deliverance brought about by Christ in the Holy Spirit."[2]

All of creation, humanity included, will come to live in a new way—the way God intended from the beginning. God's kingdom will come, and His Will *will* be done on earth as it is in Heaven. I am not referring to the end of the world but a time of great grace and liberation in which Satan will no longer be in control. We are so blessed to be living in this time, so we must know our true identities, trust God completely, and desire to live in His perfect Will—the safest place to be. Good things are coming to those who can remain faithful.

I have also included a few prayers that can be used against the enemy for deliverance:

St Anthony's Brief 3
> Behold the Cross of the Lord!
> Fly, ye powers of darkness!
> The Lion of the tribe of Judah,
> the root of David, has conquered.
> Alleluia! (Rev. 5:5)

Deliverance Prayer *(to be used on self)*
In the name of the Lord Jesus Christ, by the power of His Cross, His Blood and His Resurrection, I bind you Satan, spirits, powers and forces of darkness, the netherworld and the evil forces of nature. I take authority over all curses, hexes, demonic activity and spells directed against me, my relationships, ministry, air space, finances, and the work of my hands; I break them by the power and authority of our Lord Jesus Christ. I bind all demonic interaction, interplay and communications between spirits sent against me, and send them directly to Jesus Christ for Him to deal with as He wills. I ask forgiveness for and denounce all negative inner vows that I have made with the enemy, and I ask that Jesus Christ release me from these vows (sins) and from any bondage they may have held in me. I ask Jesus the Son of the Living God, to pour His shed Blood over every aspect of my life for my protection. I pray these things in the precious name of my Lord and Savior Jesus Christ. *Amen.*

Prayer of Command *(to be used for others)*
In His name by the power of His Cross and Blood I ask Jesus to bind any evil spirits, forces and powers of the earth, air, water, of the netherworld and the satanic forces in nature. By the power of the Holy Spirit and by His authority, I ask Jesus Christ to break any curses, hexes, or spells and send them back to where they came from. I ask you, Lord Jesus, to protect us by pouring Your Precious Blood on us, which You shed for us, and I ask You to command that any departing spirits leave quietly, without disturbance and go straight to the foot of Your Cross to dispose of as You see fit. I ask You to bind any demonic interaction, interplay or communications. I place *[N. (person, place or thing)]* under the protection of the Blood of Jesus Christ which He shed for us. *Amen.*

A Prayer for Healing

Heavenly Father, I thank you for loving me. I thank you for sending your Son, Our Lord Jesus Christ, to the world to save and to set me free. I trust in your power and grace that sustain and restore me.

Loving Father, touch me now with your healing hands, for I believe that your will is for me to be well in mind, body, soul and spirit. Cover me with the most precious blood of your Son, our Lord Jesus Christ from the top of my head to the soles of my feet. Cast out anything that should not be in me. Root out any unhealthy and abnormal cells. Open any blocked arteries or veins and rebuild and replenish any damaged areas. Remove all inflammation and cleanse any infection by the power of Jesus' precious blood.

Let the fire of your healing love pass through my entire body to heal and make new any diseased areas so that my body will function the way you created it to function. Touch also my mind and my emotion, even the deepest recesses of my heart.

Heal the hurts and pains and all the wounds that I have in my life. Saturate my entire being with your presence, love, joy, and peace and draw me ever closer to you every moment of my life. And Father, fill me with your Holy Spirit and empower me to do your works so that my life will bring glory and honor to your holy name. I ask this in the name of the Lord Jesus Christ. *Amen.*[4]

As a Catholic, I have found a worldwide community of Christians, ordained and lay alike, who pray in unity for personal deliverance and for that of our families, communities, and nations.

The site is www.auxiliumchristianorum.org.

Thus says the Lord to you, "Fear not, and be not dismayed at this great multitude; for the battle is not yours but God's." (2 Chron. 20:15)

**I trust that God will protect me.
I trust that He will never allow anything
unless it can be for my victory.**

CHAPTER 10

On Trust

All I have seen teaches me to trust the creator for all I have not seen.
-Ralph Waldo Emerson

We trust people all the time. When my doctor hands me a diagnosis or prescription, I trust he knows what he is doing. When I get on a plane, I trust the airline has hired competent pilots. Generally, we trust based on experience. If we can trust people who do not necessarily love us, why do we have such a difficult time trusting God, who loves us so much that He gave His very life for love of us?

God won't mislead us or pull a "bait and switch." He does not forget or break promises (Num. 23:19). He is faithful, trustworthy, and omniscient—He knows everything! He knows our future choices. Because He knows more than we, He can help us avoid the things that are not in our best interests; we must simply allow Him to do so.

Scripture reminds us over and over to trust God: "Trust in the Lord with all your heart, and do not lean on your own understanding" (Prov. 3:5). But what does *trust* actually mean? To trust the Lord means to have confidence in Him, to have faith in His promises; it stems from an intimate relationship with Him.

Although *faith* and *trust* are used interchangeably, they are different. *Faith* is used in the sense of "belief" or "devotion." For example, in Luke 7:1–10, the centurion did not have a relationship with Jesus, but he had the belief—the faith—that Jesus had the power to heal his servant. *Trust* is used in the sense of "confidence" and "reliance." In Genesis 22:1–9, both Isaac, who is put on the altar as a sacrifice, and Abraham demonstrate an incredible level of trust. Both of these acts of profound trust were rooted in a very personal relationship.

Generally, believing blindly in someone or something is about faith, not trust. Trust is not blind; it is built. It is earned and can be strengthened or weakened over time based on one's experiences. For example, think of a marriage: If the spouses are faithful, trust is built, but if not, trust is compromised or broken. Trust is mostly used in the context of personal relationships, based on the integrity, skills, assurances, strengths, and capabilities of others.

Trusting God can be as simple as truly believing that He is *good* and grasping the fact that He totally loves us. If we truly believe in His love, that He wants only the best and highest good for us, trust can develop. We can trust God even more if we understand that He has the *power* to help and *wants* to help. In both my spiritual growth and healing, I have found this to be the foundational secret: *The more we trust, the more He will do for us.*

Many Biblical figures struggled to trust God's plan. We will take a look at some of them because we likely relate to their struggles.

Eve

So when the woman saw that the tree was good for food, and that it was a delight to the eyes, and that the tree was to be desired to make one wise, she took of its fruit and ate. (Gen. 3:6)

Why would Eve disobey God if she had everything she could have ever wanted? Eve gives in to the temptation of doubting God's goodness. She becomes suspicious of Him and feels He is holding out on her; she does not trust God is going to look out for her best interests. She wants to know as much as God knows, so she can take care of herself in case God lets her down. God wants us to release our need to know and instead trust in Him with the plan for our lives.

Sarah

Now Abraham and Sarah were old, advanced in age; it had ceased to be with Sarah after the manner of women. So Sarah laughed to herself, saying, "After I have grown old, and my husband is old, shall I have pleasure?" (Gen. 18:11–12)

Like Sarah as she hoped for a child past her childbearing age, we can struggle to trust God's plan because the situation seems impossible. We are told to "lean not on [our] own understanding" (Prov. 3:5) because He can do things beyond our frail human understanding.

Hagar

When the water in the skin was gone, she cast the child under one of the bushes. Then she went, and sat down over against him a good way off, about the distance of a bowshot; for she said, "Let me not look upon the death of the child." (Gen. 21:15–16)

Years before, God makes Hagar a promise: "I will greatly multiply your descendants so that they will be too many to count" (Gen. 16:10 [NASB]). Now, she struggles to hold onto hope. Hagar does not trust God to honor His promise. Like Hagar, we may doubt God's promises because we put a timetable on them and become frustrated when He does not move things according to our schedule.

Rachel

When Rachel saw that she bore Jacob no children, she envied her sister; and she said to Jacob, "Give me children, or I shall die!" (Gen. 30:1)

Rachel is desperate for a child, but instead of trusting God with her desire, she takes control, giving Jacob another woman to bear her children. The control freak in us can relate to Rachel: "If God isn't moving," we may think, "I will make a move." We think we know how to run our lives better than God.

Also, Rachel seems to be making an idol out of her desire for a child. So often, we want something so badly that we put it in front of God—giving it all of our time, attention, resources, and even our heart.

Job's Wife

Then his wife said to him, "Do you still hold fast your integrity? Curse God, and die." (Job 2:9)

Job's wife may have responded so coldly to her husband's plight because it is too difficult to watch. When we watch someone we love struggle with a debilitating illness, for example, we may feel helpless, afraid, and sometimes even angry at God. Job's wife does not trust God to help her husband through this trial, wondering why God would allow something so terrible to happen. She fails to trust that God is still there, that he had not abandoned her husband; without a full understanding of the bigger picture, she stops trusting God.

Elijah

In 1 Kings 18–19, Elijah is so afraid of Jezebel that he runs into the desert and prays for death. He does not trust God to take care of him, even after he just saw God work an incredible miracle on Mount Carmel and slaughter the prophets of Baal. Like Elijah, we often forget the times God has helped us out of difficult situations and run away from—rather than into—His loving arms.

The Israelites

For the people of Israel walked forty years in the wilderness, till all the nation, the men of war that came forth out of Egypt, perished, because they did not hearken to the voice of the Lord; to them the Lord swore that he would not let them see the land which the Lord had sworn to their fathers to give us, a land flowing with milk and honey. (Josh. 5:6)

God brings the Israelites out of Egypt, parts the Red Sea, feeds them manna, never lets their shoes wear out, gives them guidance . . . and they still will not trust God! The Israelites then wandered in the desert for forty years and never got to enter the Promised Land because of their lack of trust. Like the Israelites, are we obstinate in our sin, stubborn in our own will? Do we place so little value on what He has already given us and still wants to give us? Do we complain about everything while overlooking God's blessings? Do we take Him for granted? Do we murmur, or do we thank God for His providence?

Judas

When Judas, his betrayer, saw that he was condemned, he repented and brought back the thirty pieces of silver to the chief priests and the elders, saying, "I have sinned in betraying innocent blood." They said, "What is that to us? See to it yourself." And throwing down the pieces of silver in the temple, he departed; and he went and hanged himself. (Matt. 27:3–5)

Judas does not trust in God's mercy. He thinks his sin is unforgiveable and falls into despair. Although he knows Jesus, he does not *know* and trust Him. Like Judas, we can be tempted to despair or give into self-pity. Maybe we even believe our sin is greater than God's love.

So many of God's people struggled to trust Him. If we are honest with ourselves, we will admit we do the same. In many moments of my life, I could identify with these stories. Even now, when I think I have finally learned to trust God's goodness or providence, some challenge will surface, and I fall flat on my face again. I have learned to run to God, asking Him to forgive me for not trusting Him as I should. Throughout this journey, I have learned that the more I trust Him, the more He works in my life. When I give Him the little trust I can muster, He outdoes me in giving more than I could have hoped for. Similarly, many people in the Bible prove the power of trusting in God.

Abraham

By faith Abraham, when he was called to go out into a place which he should after receive for an inheritance, he obeyed; and went out, not knowing where he went. By faith he sojourned in the land of promise, as in a strange country, dwelling in tabernacles with Isaac and Jacob, the heirs with him of the same promise. (Heb. 11:8)

Many times, Abraham demonstrates great trust in God. He follows God. Even though he is unsure where he is going, he trusts and follows the Lord's leading. Then, although he and his wife, Sarah, are well past childbearing age, he trusts God's promise that the Redeemer would come through his family. In his greatest act of trust, God asks Abraham to sacrifice his only son, Isaac, even though God had just promised that Abraham's descendants would be a great nation. Still, he trusted! We can see from these stories that if we trust, even when God seems to be asking us to bear the unimaginable, He will take care of us better than we could imagine.

Joshua

Joshua's story—found in the books of Exodus, Numbers, and Joshua—demonstrates trust in God's plan, as well. After Moses leads the Israelites out of Egypt, they come to the edge of the Promised Land. Preparing to enter the land, Moses sends twelve spies to learn how best to conquer. The spies bring back news that the land is as good as God promised; however, ten of the spies report giants are in the land and the Israelites could not be victorious in battle. These ten had no faith in the God who had miraculously delivered them from Egypt.

However, the two remaining spies—Joshua and Caleb—are the only two adults who enter the Promised Land forty years later. Joshua eventually becomes the leader of Israel. Because of his relationship with God, He leads the Israelites to destroy the city of Jericho (Josh. 6:20). The walls of Jericho fall because of Joshua's trust in God.

Esther

In the Book of Esther, when Persian King Ahasuerus seeks a new wife after his queen refused to obey him, he chooses Esther for her beauty. The king's chief advisor, Haman, is offended by Mordecai, Esther's cousin and guardian; Haman gets permission to have all of the Jews in the kingdom killed. Esther foils the plan and wins permission for the Jews to kill their enemies. Esther trusts God, even with her very life, to guide her and save her people.

Gideon

In the Book of Judges, Gideon is one of the judges chosen to speak God's Word in the Promised Land before they are given a king. He eventually leads Israel into battle against the Midianites, who have more than four times the number of fighting men. God tells Gideon the Israelites have too many men—He wants people to know that God, not merely a large army, is the one who won the battle—and whittles the number down to just three hundred. Although Gideon is scared, he trusts God to prove His promise and conquers the Midianites.

Noah

By faith Noah, being warned by God concerning events as yet un-seen, took heed and constructed an ark for the saving of his household; by this he condemned the world and became an heir of the right-eousness which comes by faith. (Heb. 11:7)

When Noah hears God's warning about the flood, Noah believes Him. He wastes no time and, for 120 years, he works on the ark with no sign of rain. Noah's belief in God directly contrasts the sin and disbelief of the rest of the world; because of his faith, he saves his family and be-comes one of the greatest examples of trusting God, even when seem-ingly ludicrous.

Moses

Moses is the only person in the Bible to speak to God face-to-face; other prophets experience God only through visions and dreams. Though he begins with a lot of questions for God, Moses ends up trusting to heroic degrees. Like many of us, Moses believes himself unsuitable for God's requests and wonders why God chooses him. When Moses finally trusts God instead of himself, he becomes one of the greatest heroes in the Bible.

Mary and Joseph

When Mary receives Gabriel's message about Jesus's conception through the Holy Spirit, she likely feels overwhelmed: She knows the potential problems of being a virgin and unwed mother. Despite uncer-tainties and questions, she chooses to trust God's divine plan for her life and surrenders her will completely so that God's will could manifest in her life. Mary's trust in God is greater than her concerns for the future.

Despite the questions she likely had about Joseph—Would he believe her? Would he be angry? Would he still marry her? Would she have to raise a baby alone if he rejects her?—she chooses to trust that God can work out every problem she encounters if she submits unques-tioningly to His will.

Joseph, too, trusts—in God *and* in Mary. His betrothed tells him she is pregnant with God's baby, so he turns to God in his confusion. The angel advises him to "take Mary as his wife" (Matt. 1:20); without further question, he does as he is told (Matt. 1:24). Through his constant trust in God's guidance, he remains the model of an ideal husband and father.

Throughout their lives, they need to trust many times: They give birth in a stable and then, in the greatest act of trust, Mary trusts God when she gives her only son to die—watching Him be tortured and killed and trusting that God would raise Him again.

Jesus

Jesus completely trusts His Heavenly Father, even to the point of death on a cross. The scourging, the crucifixion, the pain of seeing His mother suffer—He became sin for us. On the cross, He cries out, "My God, my God, why hast thou forsaken me?" Although we may read this plea and believe He feels abandoned, the Jews living at that time would have known He is referencing Psalm 22. Those standing there would have known the lines that follow:

> They open wide their mouths at me
> As a ravening and a roaring lion.
> I am poured out like water,
> And all my bones are out of joint;
> My heart is like wax;
> It is melted within me.
> My strength is dried up like a potsherd,
> And my tongue cleaves to my jaws;
> And You lay me in the dust of death.
> For dogs have surrounded me;
> A band of evildoers has encompassed me;
> They pierced my hands and my feet.
> I can count all my bones.
> They look, they stare at me;
> They divide my garments among them,
> And for my clothing they cast lots. (Ps. 22:13–18 [NASB])

Jesus is calling them to understand the psalm is talking about Him, invoking the psalm as a prayer to reveal what those crucifying Him fail to see. This psalm is an expression of hope that God will bring an end to the persecution and suffering He is enduring. It is a declaration of a prophetic fulfillment: Through Jesus's death on the cross, vindication will follow. God's power will manifest over his enemies and draw people into relationship with their God. Thus, Jesus is the ultimate example of trusting God, even amid the impossible.

As we begin to ponder how God is asking us to trust Him, we should remember that God asked some other Biblical figures to trust in some pretty strange ways:

- Isaiah walks around town naked for three years, shocking the whole neighborhood. (Isa. 20:2–3)
- Abraham has to make sure he and all his descendants cut off their foreskin. *Ouch!* (Gen. 17:9–11)
- Ezekiel has to lie on his left side for 390 days, then on his right side for forty more before baring his arm and prophesying against Jerusalem. (Ezek. 1)
- Ezekiel is told to cook bread over a fire of human dung, but he bargains with God to use cow dung instead because human excrement is considered unclean while a cow's is normal fuel. So there is some Bible history for that Ezekiel bread in grocery stores! (Ezek. 4:9–15)
- Ezekiel has to shave his head and beard and weigh the hairs. He is told to burn one third, hack one third with a sword, and scatter one third to the wind. (Ezek. 5:1–2)
- Jeremiah has to wear and then bury his underwear. (Jer. 13:4)
- Elijah eats from a bird. When God sends a drought as punishment to the nation of Israel, he sends Elijah to hide in a cave. There, he eats food provided to him by ravens until the time comes to share God's message. (1 Kings 17:1–5)
- Hosea is ordered to marry the most promiscuous woman he can find "for like an adulterous wife this land is guilty of unfaithfulness to the Lord." (Hosea 1:2)
- Hosea then names two of his kids "I have no pity" and "Not my people." His daughter has to be called "Not loved"—a perfect way to give a kid a rough start in life. (Hosea 1:4–9)

I recently heard a priest say that trust is the foundation of a relationship with God; lack of trust was the original sin: "Man, tempted by the devil, let his trust in his Creator die in his heart and, abusing his freedom, disobeyed God's command. This is what man's first sin consisted of. All subsequent sin would be disobedience toward God and lack of trust in his goodness" (CCC 397). Reading over these examples of those who failed to trust God and those who did, we should begin to ask ourselves where we fall on the spectrum and where we allow our lack of trust in God to lead us toward temptation and away from Him.

A Personal Story of Trust

I had been suffering tremendously with back pain that disabled me and stripped me of my life as I knew it. For most of my journey, I did not trust God or anyone else very much, even though I thought I did. I did not see my own part in my pain but believed God had let me down, that my suffering was his fault.

I felt pretty "saintly": I attended daily mass and confessed my sins frequently. I read every book about healing I could get my hands on, and I could not find any reason I was not healed. Although I read a few authors with the charism of healing who suggested sin as a block, I believed I did not have any major sin in my life.

I prayed to God to reveal why I felt stuck, why I was not healing. I received a word of knowledge: God wanted me to show Him my love for Him by trusting Him completely. If I could do so, I would be relieved of my unbearable suffering. The two issues I needed to address were obedience and conversion, two issues I thought I had already mastered. God specifically told me, "You place many *things* before me; you cling to earthly things more than you do me." He wanted certain sins, such as my spiritual pride and control issues, gone.

He specifically told me what He expected of me. I was shocked and begged God to grant me a sign—something I seldom, if ever, ask for—if this message was truly from Him. I asked for a rainbow, a sign of promise, knowing the dry weather conditions and darkness would make the request a miracle. I was in so much pain that I could not have gotten out of bed to see the sky, even if I had wanted to. I cried myself to sleep.

The next morning, I heard on the news that a rare aurora borealis had appeared in the sky, coincidentally during the time I had prayed the previous evening. It was described as a rainbow of color. Such a sighting is an almost impossible occurrence for Buffalo, New York; if we do see this phenomenon, it is in shades of green or blue, never a rainbow. Then came the hard part: trusting God's promise with no sign of healing in my body.

For six weeks, I seemed to get worse. Multiple times a day, my hips were dislocating where my hip meets my spine. I was in constant, severe pain each time I moved. Still, I blindly trusted in His promise. "Jesus, I trust in you" became my life prayer, whether I felt it or not. I demonstrated my trust by not clinging to earthly comforts but instead holding onto Him alone and doing the specific things He asked of me.

On December 12, 2011, my hips began to stabilize. I was unaware God was at work until Christmas Day when I heard in prayer, "You have your foundation." I still could not connect all the dots until my doctor used those same words: "Your hips are your foundation." I then knew that everything was connected.

Although I was not instantly healed, God showed me a glimpse of what was to come. My physical foundation was my hips, and little did I know that God would indeed grant me this healing. My spiritual foundation was trust, which proved to be the most valuable foundation and the one the enemy feared the most from me.

That same night I heard my doctor's words and learned that God was calling me to deeper trust, I had a dream. The devil was wrestling me over a "book." He told me, "You can't have this. I won't let you have this!"

I responded, "I will not let go. You *can't* have it. You can't take it!"

"Let go, or I will hurt you," he said angrily.

Fearlessly, I replied, "I will not. I am not afraid of you anymore. I will not let go. All I have to do is call Jesus, and you are toast."

In a rage, he began to choke me. I felt like I was suffocating and being stabbed in the back. I woke screaming the name of Jesus. After catching my breath, I went to the kitchen for water around 1:30 A.M.

Suddenly, I felt a "darkness"; within seconds, the house began to fill with suffocating fumes. I couldn't see flames, but I knew a fire was in the house somewhere. The smoke grew more oppressive, and the smoke alarms went off. I got my daughter out of the house, and a picture of a breaker box flashed in my mind.

As a side note, I am not good in emergencies; I do not think clearly or rationally. I also have horrible vision and cannot read without a magnifying glass or glasses, and the switches on the breaker were not labeled. But as I got out of the house, cell phone in hand and calling 911, I hit one switch on my breaker box.

The firemen arrived fifteen minutes later. They searched but said, "There was a fire, but it seems to have stopped. Did you do anything?" I told them about hitting a breaker as I ran out of the house. They asked me to flip it back on; as soon as I did, the fire started again.

They found the fire in the refrigerator motor—a highly unusual place for a fire. After, they told me that if I had not turned the breaker off, the fire would have traveled through the appliance cord in my walls, and the house would have been gone in minutes.

What the enemy had intended for my destruction, God used to save me. I had stumbled upon a foundational key that had enraged the enemy: trust.

Of course, trust has to be lived out. Responsibility and action are required on our end. We may be called to turn away from sin, a sign we do not trust in God's goodness and love and are instead trying to control our own happiness. We may have to let go of something we are clinging to or be obedient, even when we do not see God acting according to our plan.

Abraham trusted God perfectly, but he still had to demonstrate that trust through obedience and detachment on Mount Moriah. Even Naaman had to trust and be obedient to the prophet Elisha before he received this healing. In Eden, our first parents did not trust, as demonstrated by their lack of obedience.

In my own case, God loved me too much to give me something I was not prepared to receive. He desired my complete trust before handing me the gift of healing, and I had to demonstrate this trust by believing in His promise without evidence, confronting deeper sin, and obediently saying "yes" to what he asked of me. As the years progressed, my healing came in increments; the more I trusted, the more healing— both physical and spiritual—came. More valuable to me than any physical healing, a deeper relationship with and love for Him resulted from those struggles and trials with each passing day.

I have included here the "Litany of Trust," written by Sister Faustina Maria Pia.

From the belief that I have to earn Your love
Deliver me, Jesus.
From the fear that I am unlovable
Deliver me, Jesus.
From the false security that I have what it takes
Deliver me, Jesus.
From the fear that trusting You will leave me more destitute
Deliver me, Jesus.
From all suspicion of Your words and promises
Deliver me, Jesus.
From the rebellion against childlike dependency on You
Deliver me, Jesus.
From refusals and reluctances in accepting Your will
Deliver me, Jesus.
From anxiety about the future
Deliver me, Jesus.
From resentment or excessive preoccupation with the past
Deliver me, Jesus.
From restless self-seeking in the present moment
Deliver me, Jesus.
From disbelief in Your love and presence
Deliver me, Jesus.
From the fear of being asked to give more than I have
Deliver me, Jesus.
From the belief that my life has no meaning or worth
Deliver me, Jesus.
From the fear of what love demands
Deliver me, Jesus.
From discouragement
Deliver me, Jesus.
That You are continually holding me, sustaining me, loving me
Jesus, I trust in you.
That Your love goes deeper than my sins and failings and transforms me
Jesus, I trust in you.

That not knowing what tomorrow brings is an invitation to lean on You
Jesus, I trust in you.
That you are with me in my suffering
Jesus, I trust in you.
That my suffering, united to Your own, will bear fruit in this life and the next
Jesus, I trust in you.
That You will not leave me orphan, that You are present in Your Church
Jesus, I trust in you.
That Your plan is better than anything else
Jesus, I trust in you.
That You always hear me and in Your goodness always respond to me
Jesus, I trust in you.
That You give me the grace to accept forgiveness and to forgive others
Jesus, I trust in you.
That You give me all the strength I need for what is asked
Jesus, I trust in you.
That my life is a gift
Jesus, I trust in you.
That You will teach me to trust You
Jesus, I trust in you.
That You are my Lord and my God
Jesus, I trust in you.
That I am Your beloved one
Jesus, I trust in you.
Amen.

May you trust God that you are exactly where you are meant to be.
—St. Therese of Lisieux

I trust that God has good things planned for me.
I trust that He will handle all the things I can't.
I trust that He wants me to live in freedom, peace, and joy!

CHAPTER 11

Your True Identity

*You know you're in love when you can't fall asleep because
reality is finally better than your dreams.*
-Dr. Seuss

ave you ever experienced or desired a love in which the other
person just "gets you" and understands you so deeply that you
actually seem to share one soul? Some of us may have known
this kind of love, but many have not. The Dr. Seuss quote above seems
apt for this chapter because most of us dream of a love like that. But the
most wonderful thing is . . . we can have it!

This kind of love is for each of us, not just a lucky few, to experience. God has a dream for us—a dream far better than anything we could
dream for ourselves. Why? Because He is in love with us!

What does falling in love with someone entail? We spend time
with them, find out what they like, what is important to them; we open
ourselves to those things. We tell them we love them and try to do little
things that show our love. We include them in our lives and make room
for them. We talk about them to others. We think about them constantly.

We share ourselves with them. In a perfect world, they reciprocate.

The good news is, when we fall in love with Jesus, He does reciprocate! We are God's children, heirs to His kingdom. We are fearfully and wonderfully made and are precious in His sight. We are victors and overcomers. We are valued and His beloved. We are loved so deeply just the way we are without having to earn it. We are loved simply because we *are*.

Bob Marley once expressed love like this:

Only once in your life, I truly believe, you find someone who can completely turn your world around. You tell them things that you've never shared with another soul and they absorb everything you say and actually want to hear more. You share hopes for the future, dreams that will never come true, goals that were never achieved and the many disappointments life has thrown at you. When something wonderful happens, you can't wait to tell them about it, knowing they will share in your excitement. They are not embarrassed to cry with you when you are hurting or laugh with you when you make a fool of yourself. Never do they hurt your feelings or make you feel like you are not good enough, but rather they build you up and show you the things about yourself that make you special and even beautiful. There is never any pressure, jealousy or competition but only a quiet calmness when they are around. You can be yourself and not worry about what they will think of you because they love you for who you are. The things that seem insignificant to most people such as a note, song or walk become invaluable treasures kept safe in your heart to cherish forever. Memories of your childhood come back and are so clear and vivid it's like being young again. Colors seem brighter and more brilliant. Laughter seems part of daily life where before it was infrequent or didn't exist at all. In their presence, there's no need for continuous conversation, but you find you're quite content in just having them nearby. Things that never interested you before become fascinating because you know they are important to this person who is so special to you. You think of this person on every occasion and in everything you do. Simple things bring them to mind like a pale blue sky, gentle wind or even a storm cloud on the horizon. You open your heart knowing that there's a chance it may be broken one day and in opening your heart, you experience a love and joy that you never dreamed possible. You find that being vulnerable is the only way to allow your heart to feel true pleasure that's so real it scares you. You find strength in knowing you have a true friend and possibly a soul mate who will remain loyal to the end. Life seems completely different, exciting and worthwhile. Your only hope and security is in knowing that they are a part of your life. [1]

When I first read this quote, I cried. I then reread it with the thought of Jesus as that special person. My healing journey led me to seeing that He was next to me during so many pivotal moments in my life. He was there when I was struggling. He was there to hold me at night when I was afraid. He was there when I would see a beautiful sunrise or watch a thunderstorm from my porch. He was in the blooming flowers saying, "Here, my Love. This is for you! Do you like it?" He was there listening as I poured out my heart and frustrations. He *loved* me.

I wish the same sort of love for all of us, but more importantly, God wishes this love for us, too! The first step to accepting His profound love is to recognize that we are *worth* being loved like this, believing that we can be first in someone's life or in someone's heart. The whole story of salvation is a love story about each of us. If one of us were the only person who needed to be saved, Jesus would have gone to the cross. God so loved each of us that He sent His only Son to suffer horribly and die just so we could come home and be loved by Him forever (John 3:16).

The prophet Jeremiah says, "Before I formed you in the womb I knew you, and before you were born I consecrated you" (Jer. 1:5). We were thought of before our parents conceived us. We are so important to God that He delighted in even thinking about us, and His thoughts are so perfect that just the thought of us brought us into existence. He was so excited that He wanted us to be born just so He could love us.

In fact, the entire book of Song of Songs was written about God's love for us, His Church. The book is actually a love song about the marriage relationship between Christ and His Church. He wants to be with us. When we come close to Him, His heart beats faster; when we even glance at Him, His heart beats with excitement: "You have made my heart beat faster, my sister, my bride; You have made my heart beat faster with a single glance of your eyes" (Song of Sol. 4:9 [NASB]). How sought after and special we are that even a *glance* toward God would send His heart beating with excitement!

Catholics experience this special connection with God each time we receive Communion. We walk down the aisle like a bride toward her groom. We meet him at the *baldacchino* (the canopy over the altar meant to symbolize the wedding chamber). Our bridegroom physically enters us, and we become one flesh. God loves us so much that He comes under the appearance of a tiny piece of bread just so He could physically become one with us. We are so "impregnated" with His love that we become fruitful and multiply, bringing more people into His kingdom. St. Thomas Aquinas said, "The Eucharist is the Sacrament of Love. It signifies Love; it produces Love. The Eucharist is the consummation of the whole spiritual life."[2]

Fr. Pedro Arrupe, SJ, is attributed with the following quote:

Nothing is more practical than
finding God, than
falling in Love
in a quite absolute, final way.
What you are in love with,
what seizes your imagination, will affect everything.
It will decide
what will get you out of bed in the morning,
what you do with your evenings,
how you spend your weekends,
what you read, whom you know,
what breaks your heart,
and what amazes you with joy and gratitude.
Fall in Love, stay in love,
and it will decide everything.[3]

I am ashamed to admit that I did not really love God when I first read this quote. I said I loved Him. I served Him. I went to Church. However, I realized I spent so much energy trying to love people in my life or trying to get them to love me; I did not put anywhere near that amount of effort into trying to get to know God. But then, He "wooed" me. Falling in love with Him changed everything.

When we understand and fully accept how deeply and completely we are loved, our entire outlook on healing will change. Healing will no longer be something we have to "get" from a distant God but will instead become a journey toward Him. The closer we come, the more whole we become until we are made perfect in his presence.

Some of us may still be asking, "Why am I not healed?" Hopefully, some information in these pages has proven helpful along the path to healing. Maybe now, you can see your journey is progressing but not on your timetable. Maybe you have read through these chapters and have examined your life, making necessary improvements—whether in attitude, forgiveness, or patterns of sin. Maybe you have put some of these strategies into practice, but nothing seems to have moved toward a physical healing. I offer this thought on trusting the One who loves you.

When my son was little, he fell and scraped his leg so badly that bits of stone and dirt were deeply embedded beneath his skin. The doctor tried to remove as much as he could—painstakingly washing, tweezing, and actually cutting some of the skin to get to the deeper debris. My son screamed and cried; the process seemed to take forever. Then, infection set in, and we made more trips to the doctor. The healing took almost a full year. My son could not understand why it took so long and why his leg still hurt. As a mother, my heart ached to see him suffer, but I knew that any remaining debris or dirt would prevent the wound from healing.

In my own journey, I can see how painstakingly and mercifully God was helping me. He never stopped loving me, despite my tantrums and failures. In those dark days, I grew to not only love Him but to be *in love* with Him. Going through a trial or tragedy helps us see the one standing by our side through it all. Through difficulty, a bond forms, our hearts open, and trust develops.

God wants you to be healed. His Will is that you are whole. How that happens is in His hands and heart; *you* are in His hands and heart. I truly believe that healing is an issue of timing. My journey took eighteen years; now that I have come through it, I would not change a moment of the process. I can see now how God was healing me from the inside out, lovingly and carefully cleansing me, teaching me, and restoring me.

A love relationship is mutual. It shares the good and the difficult, the pains, the joys, and the victories. God desires an intimate love affair with each of us—a love so deep and enrapturing that we are able to trust when we do not understand. We must desire that relationship, as well. We have a loving God that does have a plan for great good. As I have said throughout the book, God will do the most loving thing in the most loving way for the greatest amount of good.

My own healing journey was filled at times with doubt, confusion, anger, hurt, and impatience. But I did heal—in His time and in His way. I am so thankful for His plan because I learned so much about how to be in love with a God who was in love with me.

Do not be afraid to surrender all to God. He will never disappoint a trusting soul. He cannot be outdone. What we give Him in love and trust, He will give back in a tidal wave of blessing and joy: "Things which eye has not seen and ear has not heard and which have not entered the heart of man, all that God has prepared for those who love Him" (1 Cor. 2:9 [NASB]).

God *is* relationship—Father, Son and Holy Spirit—three persons in a relationship that makes them One in Perfect Love. Ask God to help you enter into this union, and He will. When you become part of this relationship, God can move through you, act in you, and love in you because you are part of Him.

If you have questions, ask Him. He will speak in the silence of your heart. You will be completely transformed, and your life will be a reflection and witness of not only His love but His power and mercy. The fruit, the offspring of that love relationship, will be far more excellent than anything you could ever imagine or achieve on your own.

We cannot understand the mind of God: He is sovereign, and His ways are far above our ways (Isa. 55:8–9), but His way is total love. You will never regret letting go of control and letting Him take the lead; He is in love with you and wants to see you smile. Nothing else will ever be able to fulfill your deepest longings. You will have joy, you will have peace, and you will have purpose (Col. 1:24). Then, you will be able to share your journey of healing and love with others.

God will begin to work through you in the most incredible ways. You will truly become His hands and His feet, His heartbeat of love in this world.

I am my beloved's, And his desire is for me. Come, my beloved, let us go.
(Song of Sol. 7:10–11)

**I trust that My God, the one who created me,
is passionately in love with me. He is, and always will be**

APPENDIX

Meditation of Forgiveness

Lord Jesus Christ, I ask today to forgive everyone in my life. I know that You will give me the strength to forgive, and I thank You that You love me more than I love myself and that you want happiness more than I desire it for myself.

Father, forgive me for when I blamed You or others for the times when my decisions left me unhappy and empty. Forgive me for the times when death came into the family or when I experienced hard times and financial difficulties and I became bitter and resentful toward You, thinking those were punishments sent by You. Purify my heart and mind today.

Lord, I forgive myself for my sins, faults, and failings; for pride and self-reliance; for the times I did not think I needed you, religion, or faith; for the times that I did not trust in you but instead chose to into delve in superstition, Reiki, horoscopes, or New Age practices. Today, Lord, I reject it all and choose You alone as my Lord and Savior. Please forgive me and fill me with your Holy Spirit.

Lord, please forgive me for taking Your name in vain; for not putting You first in my life; for hurting others; for getting drunk; for sins against purity, for judging others and gossiping; for the resentments and anger that I hold on to; and for other sins that are weighing on me. *[Pause]* You have forgiven me. Jesus, I forgive myself!

Lord, I am choosing to truly forgive my mother/caretaker. I forgive her for all the times she hurt me, she resented me, she was angry with me or punished me. I forgive her for the times she preferred my brothers and sisters to me. I forgive her for the times I was called names; for the times I was led to believe that I was ugly, stupid, the worst of the children; or that I cost the family a lot of money. For the times she told me I was unwanted, an accident, a mistake or not what she expected. Jesus, I forgive!

Lord, I forgive my father/caretaker. I forgive him for any non-support or any lack of love, affection, or attention. I forgive him for any lack of time, for not giving me his companionship, for the times he failed me or argued and fought with my mother or siblings. For his severe punishments, for desertion; for being away from home; for divorcing my mother or for any running around. Jesus, I forgive!

Lord, I extend forgiveness to my sisters and brothers. For lying about me, for competing for my parents' love, for hurting me, for harming me, or for making my life unpleasant in any way, Jesus, I forgive!

Lord, I forgive my spouse and children for lack of love, affection, consideration, support, attention, or communication and for those other acts or words that hurt or disturb me. Jesus, I forgive!

Lord, I forgive relatives and anyone who may have interfered in our family, who may have caused confusion or dissension or torn our family apart. For all their words, thoughts, actions or omissions which injure and cause pain, Jesus, I forgive!

Lord, help me to forgive my colleagues who are difficult or make life miserable for me. For those who push their work off on me, gossip about me, will not cooperate with me, take credit for my work, try to take my job, Jesus, I forgive!

Lord, my neighbors need to be forgiven, Lord, for all their noise and inconsideration or stirring trouble instead of peace. Jesus, I forgive!

Lord, I forgive all priests, pastors, nuns, and religious brothers; church leaders and elders; my parish, my parish ministries, and my church for their lack of support or affirmation, for treating me harshly, for a lack of friendliness, for verbal or other abuses, or for not providing for me or my family. Jesus, I forgive!

Lord, I forgive those of different religious denominations or political views who have tried to convert me, harassed me, attacked me, argued with me, or forced their views on me. Jesus, I forgive!

Lord, I forgive all professional people who have hurt me in any way: doctors, nurses, lawyers, judges, or politicians. I forgive all service people: policemen, firemen, or repairmen who have taken advantage of me in their work. Jesus, I forgive!

Lord, I forgive my employer for not paying me enough money, for not appreciating my work, for being unkind and unreasonable with me, and for not complimenting me on my work. Jesus, I forgive!

Lord, I forgive my schoolteachers and instructors of the past, as well as the present. For those who punished me, humiliated me, insulted me, or treated me unjustly, Jesus, I forgive!

Lord, I forgive my friends who have let me down, lost contact with me, failed to support me, were not available when I needed help, borrowed money and did not return it, or gossiped about me. Jesus, I forgive!

Lord, I especially pray for the grace of forgiveness for that one person in my life who has hurt me the most. *[Pause. Who comes to mind? Think of that person now, and allow Jesus to give you His grace to forgive.]* Jesus, I forgive!

Lord, I now ask for your help to forgive anyone who I consider my greatest enemy, the one who is the hardest to forgive, or the one I said I will never forgive. *[Pause. Who comes to mind? Think of that person, and allow Jesus to give you His grace to forgive.]* Jesus, I forgive! I choose to forgive. Help me fully forgive.

Lord, I am especially sorry for *[Think of a time when you hurt someone. There may be multiple people who come to mind. Repeat as far back as your memory will take you. Let the Lord into your heart and mind. Give it all to Him; unload the boulder from your shoulders and cast it to the ground. Let the Lord know you no longer want it. Let the Lord in His mercy and love take it from you.]* Please forgive me for all the pain and hurt I have inflicted on others, especially *[Pause. Who comes to mind? Whom have I hurt? Think of that person now and allow Jesus to give you His grace to forgive.]* Jesus, I forgive myself!

Scriptures on Healing [ESV]

"Heal me, O Lord, and I shall be healed; save me, and I shall be saved, for you are my praise." (Jer. 17:14)

"Fear not, for I am with you; be not dismayed, for I am your God; I will strengthen you, I will help you, I will uphold you with my righteous right hand." (Isa. 41:10)

"He himself bore our sins in his body on the tree, that we might die to sin and live to righteousness. By his wounds you have been healed." (1 Pet. 2:24)

"Behold, I will bring to it health and healing, and I will heal them and reveal to them abundance of prosperity and security." (Jer. 33:6)

"But he was wounded for our transgressions; he was crushed for our iniquities; upon him was the chastisement that brought us peace, and with his stripes we are healed." (Isa. 53:5)

"And the prayer of faith will save the one who is sick, and the Lord will raise him up. And if he has committed sins, he will be forgiven." (James 5:15)

"He heals the brokenhearted and binds up their wounds." (Ps. 147:3)

"The Lord sustains him on his sickbed; in his illness you restore him to full health." (Ps. 41:3)

"Beloved, I pray that all may go well with you and that you may be in good health, as it goes well with your soul." (3 John 1:2)

"Therefore, confess your sins to one another and pray for one another, that you may be healed. The prayer of a righteous person has great power as it is working." (James 5:16)

"A joyful heart is good medicine, but a crushed spirit dries up the bones." (Prov. 17:22)

"And he called to him his twelve disciples and gave them authority over unclean spirits, to cast them out, and to heal every disease and every affliction." (Matt. 10:1)

"Is anyone among you sick? Let him call for the elders of the church, and let them pray over him, anointing him with oil in the name of the Lord." (James 5:14)

"My son, be attentive to my words; incline your ear to my sayings. Let them not escape from your sight; keep them within your heart. For they are life to those who find them, and healing to all their flesh." (Prov. 4:20–22)

"For I will restore health to you, and your wounds I will heal, declares the Lord, because they have called you an outcast: 'It is Zion, for whom no one cares!'" (Jer. 30:17)

"And the Lord will take away from you all sickness, and none of the evil diseases of Egypt, which you knew, will he inflict on you, but he will lay them on all who hate you." (Deut. 7:15)

"Heal the sick, raise the dead, cleanse lepers, cast out demons. You received without paying; give without pay." (Matt. 10:8)

"And my God will supply every need of yours according to his riches in glory in Christ Jesus." (Phil. 4:19)

"Do not be anxious about anything, but in everything by prayer and supplication with thanksgiving let your requests be made known to God. And the peace of God, which surpasses all understanding, will guard your hearts and your minds in Christ Jesus." (Phil. 4:6–7)

"Saying, 'If you will diligently listen to the voice of the Lord your God, and do that which is right in his eyes, and give ear to his command- ments and keep all his statutes, I will put none of the diseases on you that I put on the Egyptians, for I am the Lord, your healer.'" (Exod. 15:26)

"While you stretch out your hand to heal, and signs and wonders are performed through the name of your holy servant Jesus." (Acts 4:30)

"Be gracious to me, O Lord, for I am languishing; heal me, O Lord, for my bones are troubled." (Ps. 6:1)

"No weapon that is fashioned against you shall succeed, and you shall confute every tongue that rises against you in judgment. This is the heritage of the servants of the Lord and their vindication from me, declares the Lord." (Isa. 54:17)

"And without faith it is impossible to please him, for whoever would draw near to God must believe that he exists and that he rewards those who seek him." (Heb. 11:6)

"Trust in the Lord with all your heart, and do not lean on your own understanding. In all your ways acknowledge him, and he will make straight your paths. Be not wise in your own eyes; fear the Lord, and turn away from evil. It will be healing to your flesh and refreshment to your bones." (Prov. 3:5–8)

"Gracious words are like a honeycomb, sweetness to the soul and health to the body." (Prov. 16:24)

"He sent out his word and healed them, and delivered them from their destruction." (Ps. 107:20)

"More than that, we rejoice in our sufferings, knowing that suffering produces endurance, and endurance produces character, and character produces hope." (Rom. 5:3-4)

"The Spirit of the Lord is upon me, because he has anointed me to proclaim good news to the poor. He has sent me to proclaim liberty to the captives and recovering of sight to the blind, to set at liberty those who are oppressed." (Luke 4:18)

"Come to me, all who labor and are heavy laden, and I will give you rest." (Matt. 11:28)

"The thief comes only to steal and kill and destroy. I came that they may have life and have it abundantly." (John 10:10)

"And he went throughout all Galilee, teaching in their synagogues and proclaiming the gospel of the kingdom and healing every disease and every affliction among the people." (Matt. 4:23)

"Submit yourselves therefore to God. Resist the devil, and he will flee from you." (James 4:7)

"Heal the sick in it and say to them, 'The kingdom of God has come near to you.'" (Luke 10:9)

"Jesus Christ is the same yesterday and today and forever." (Heb. 13:8)

"I have seen his ways, but I will heal him; I will lead him and restore comfort to him and his mourners, creating the fruit of the lips. 'Peace, peace, to the far and to the near,' says the Lord, 'and I will heal him.'" (Isa. 57:18–19)

"But he said to me, 'My grace is sufficient for you, for my power is made perfect in weakness.' Therefore I will boast all the more gladly of my weaknesses, so that the power of Christ may rest upon me." (2 Cor. 12:9)

"Bless the Lord, O my soul, and forget not all his benefits, who forgives all your iniquity, who heals all your diseases, who redeems your life from the pit, who crowns you with steadfast love and mercy, who satisfies you with good so that your youth is renewed like the eagle's." (Ps. 103:2–5)

"I have seen his ways, but I will heal him; I will lead him and restore comfort to him and his mourners." (Isa. 57:18)

"If my people who are called by my name humble themselves, and pray and seek my face and turn from their wicked ways, then I will hear from heaven and will forgive their sin and heal their land." (2 Chron. 7:14)

"As for me, I said, 'O Lord, be gracious to me; heal me, for I have sinned against you!'" (Acts 10:38)

"How God anointed Jesus of Nazareth with the Holy Spirit and with power. He went about doing good and healing all who were oppressed by the devil, for God was with him." (Ps. 41:4)

"For we walk by faith, not by sight." (2 Cor. 5:7)

"Now faith is the assurance of things hoped for, the conviction of things not seen." (Heb. 11:1)

"See now that I, even I, am he, and there is no god beside me; I kill and I make alive; I wound and I heal; and there is none that can deliver out of my hand." (Deut. 32:39)

"And Jesus went throughout all the cities and villages, teaching in their synagogues and proclaiming the gospel of the kingdom and healing every disease and every affliction." (Matt. 9:35)

"Now therefore stand still and see this great thing that the Lord will do before your eyes." (1 Sam. 12:16)

"This is my comfort in my affliction, that your promise gives me life." (Ps. 119:50)

"I will not die but live, and will proclaim what the LORD has done." (Ps. 118:17)

"When Jesus saw her, he called her over and said to her, 'Woman, you are freed from your disability.'" (Luke 13:12)

"For to this you have been called, because Christ also suffered for you, leaving you an example, so that you might follow in his steps. He committed no sin, neither was deceit found in his mouth. When he was reviled, he did not revile in return; when he suffered, he did not threaten, but continued entrusting himself to him who judges justly. He himself bore our sins in his body on the tree, that we might die to sin and live to righteousness. By his wounds you have been healed." (1 Pet. 2:21–24)

"Is anyone among you sick? Let him call for the elders of the church, and let them pray over him, anointing him with oil in the name of the Lord. And the prayer of faith will save the one who is sick, and the Lord will raise him up. And if he has committed sins, he will be forgiven." (James 5:14–15)

"I appeal to you therefore, brothers, by the mercies of God, to present your bodies as a living sacrifice, holy and acceptable to God, which is your spiritual worship. Do not be conformed to this world, but be transformed by the renewal of your mind, that by testing you may discern what is the will of God, what is good and acceptable and perfect." (Rom. 12:1–2)

"Peace I leave with you; my peace I give to you. Not as the world gives do I give to you. Let not your hearts be troubled, neither let them be afraid." (John 14:27)

"O Lord my God, I cried to you for help, and you have healed me." (Ps. 30:2)

"He said to them, 'Because of your little faith. For truly, I say to you, if you have faith like a grain of mustard seed, you will say to this mountain, "Move from here to there," and it will move, and nothing will be impossible for you.'" (Matt. 17:20)

"On one of those days, as he was teaching, Pharisees and teachers of the law were sitting there, who had come from every village of Galilee and Judea and from Jerusalem. And the power of the Lord was with him to heal." (Luke 5:17)

"And he said to her, 'Daughter, your faith has made you well; go in peace.'" (Luke 8:48)

"And Moses cried to the Lord, 'O God, please heal her—please.'" (Num. 12:13)

"Who has believed what he has heard from us? And to whom has the arm of the Lord been revealed? For he grew up before him like a young plant, and like a root out of dry ground; he had no form or majesty that we should look at him, and no beauty that we should desire him. He was despised and rejected by men; a man of sorrows, and acquainted with grief; and as one from whom men hide their faces he was despised, and we esteemed him not. Surely he has borne our griefs and carried our sorrows; yet we esteemed him stricken, smitten by God, and afflicted. But he was wounded for our transgressions; he was crushed for our iniquities; upon him was the chastisement that brought us peace, and with his stripes we are healed." (Isa. 53:1–12)

"But for you who fear my name, the sun of righteousness shall rise with healing in its wings. You shall go out leaping like calves from the stall." (Mal. 4:2)

"You shall serve the Lord your God, and he will bless your bread and your water, and I will take sickness away from among you." (Exod. 23:25)

"And he said to her, 'Daughter, your faith has made you well; go in peace, and be healed of your disease.'" (Mark 5:34)

"Then he said to the man, 'Stretch out your hand.' And the man stretched it out, and it was restored, healthy like the other." (Matt. 12:13)

"Blessed is the one who considers the poor! In the day of trouble the Lord delivers him; the Lord protects him and keeps him alive; he is called blessed in the land; you do not give him up to the will of his enemies. The Lord sustains him on his sickbed; in his illness you restore him to full health." (Ps. 41:1–3)

"And Peter said to him, 'Aeneas, Jesus Christ heals you; rise and make your bed.' And immediately he rose." (Acts 9:34)

"So we do not lose heart. Though our outer self is wasting away, our inner self is being renewed day by day. For this light momentary affliction is preparing for us an eternal weight of glory beyond all comparison, as we look not to the things that are seen but to the things that are unseen. For the things that are seen are transient, but the things that are unseen are eternal." (1 Cor. 4:16–18)

"Behold, blessed is the one whom God reproves; therefore despise not the discipline of the Almighty. For he wounds, but he binds up; he shatters, but his hands heal." (Job 5:17–18)

"Blessed be the God and Father of our Lord Jesus Christ, the Father of mercies and God of all comfort." (2 Cor. 1:3)

"For everything there is a season, and a time for every matter under heaven: a time to be born, and a time to die; a time to plant, and a time to pluck up what is planted; a time to kill, and a time to heal; a time to break down, and a time to build up." (Eccles. 3:1–3)

"And he laid his hands on her, and immediately she was made straight, and she glorified God." (Luke 13:13)

"'Creating the fruit of the lips. Peace, peace, to the far and to the near,' says the Lord, 'and I will heal him.'" (Isa. 57:19)

"Behold, we consider those blessed who remained steadfast. You have heard of the steadfastness of Job, and you have seen the purpose of the Lord, how the Lord is compassionate and merciful." (James 5:11)

"When the crowds learned it, they followed him, and he welcomed them and spoke to them of the kingdom of God and cured those who had need of healing." (Luke 9:11)

"For this people's heart has grown dull, and with their ears they can barely hear, and their eyes they have closed, lest they should see with their eyes and hear with their ears and understand with their heart and turn, and I would heal them." (Matt. 13:15)

"To another faith by the same Spirit, to another gifts of healing by the one Spirit." (1 Cor. 12:9)

"This poor man cried, and the Lord heard him and saved him out of all his troubles." (Ps. 34:6)

"It is good for me that I was afflicted, that I might learn your statutes." (Ps. 119:71)

"The Lord make his face to shine upon you and be gracious to you; the Lord lift up his countenance upon you and give you peace. 'So shall they put my name upon the people of Israel, and I will bless them.'" (Num. 6:25–27)

"And the Lord will strike Egypt, striking and healing, and they will return to the Lord, and he will listen to their pleas for mercy and heal them." (Isa. 19:22)

"For as the rain and the snow come down from heaven and do not return there but water the earth, making it bring forth and sprout, giving seed to the sower and bread to the eater, so shall my word be that goes out from my mouth; it shall not return to me empty, but it shall accomplish that which I purpose, and shall succeed in the thing for which I sent it." (Isa. 55:10–11)

"Surely he has borne our griefs and carried our sorrows; yet we esteemed him stricken, smitten by God, and afflicted. But he was wounded for our transgressions; he was crushed for our iniquities; upon him was the chastisement that brought us peace, and with his stripes we are healed." (Isa. 53:4–5)

"Be gracious to me, O Lord, for I am in distress; my eye is wasted from grief; my soul and my body also." (Ps. 31:9)

"Then shall your light break forth like the dawn, and your healing shall spring up speedily; your righteousness shall go before you; the glory of the Lord shall be your rear guard." (Isa. 58:8)

"When he went ashore he saw a great crowd, and he had compassion on them and healed their sick." (Matt. 14:14)

"I am severely afflicted; give me life, O Lord, according to your word!" (Ps. 119:107)

"Let those who delight in my righteousness shout for joy and be glad and say evermore, 'Great is the Lord, who delights in the welfare of his servant!'" (Ps. 35:27)

"For this people's heart has grown dull, and with their ears they can barely hear, and their eyes they have closed; lest they should see with their eyes and hear with their ears and understand with their heart and turn, and I would heal them." (Acts 28:27)

"He has blinded their eyes and hardened their heart, lest they see with their eyes, and understand with their heart, and turn, and I would heal them." (John 12:40)

"Behold, I have given you authority to tread on serpents and scorpions, and over all the power of the enemy, and nothing shall hurt you. Nevertheless, do not rejoice in this, that the spirits are subject to you, but rejoice that your names are written in heaven." (Luke 10:19–20)

"Be not wise in your own eyes; fear the Lord, and turn away from evil. It will be healing to your flesh and refreshment to your bones." (Prov. 3:7–8)

"Therefore I did not presume to come to you. But say the word, and let my servant be healed." (Luke 7:7)

"And he did not do many mighty works there, because of their unbelief." (Matt. 13:58)

"Judge not, that you be not judged. For with the judgment you pronounce you will be judged, and with the measure you use it will be measured to you. Why do you see the speck that is in your brother's eye, but do not notice the log that is in your own eye? Or how can you say to your brother, 'Let me take the speck out of your eye,' when there is the log in your own eye? You hypocrite, first take the log out of your own eye, and then you will see clearly to take the speck out of your brother's eye." (Matt. 7:1–29)

"Turn back, and say to Hezekiah the leader of my people, 'Thus says the Lord, the God of David your father: I have heard your prayer; I have seen your tears. Behold, I will heal you. On the third day you shall go up to the house of the Lord.'" (2 Kings 20:5)

"Truly I say to you, whoever says to this mountain, 'Be taken up and cast into the sea,' and does not doubt in his heart, but believes that what he says is going to happen, it will be granted him. Therefore I say to you, all things for which you pray and ask, believe that you have received them, and they will be granted you." (Mark 11:23–24)

"The thief comes only to steal and kill and destroy; I came that they may have life, and have it abundantly." (John 10:10)

"This is the confidence which we have before Him, that, if we ask anything according to His will, He hears us. And if we know that He hears us in whatever we ask, we know that we have the requests which we have asked from Him." (1 John 5:14–15)

"But if the Spirit of Him who raised Jesus from the dead dwells in you, He who raised Christ from the dead will also give life to your mortal bodies through His Spirit who dwells in you." (Rom. 8:11)

"And Jesus went about all the cities and villages, teaching in their synagogues and preaching the gospel of the kingdom, and healing every disease and every infirmity. When he saw the crowds, he had compassion for them, because they were harassed and helpless, like sheep without a shepherd. (Joel 3:10b) Let the weakling say, 'I am strong!'" (Matt. 9:35)

"The joy of the LORD is your strength." (Neh. 8:10)

"I can do all things through Christ who strengthens me." (Phil. 4:13)

"And the God of all grace, who called you to his eternal glory in Christ, after you have suffered a little while, will himself restore you and make you strong, firm and steadfast." (1 Pet. 5:10)

"Greater is he that is in you than he that is in the world." (1 John 4:4b [KJ V])

Chapter 7

I have included here an overview of the hindrances to healing, as well as accompanying Scriptural passages to meditate on.

Issues related to faith
- Unbelief (Matt. 17:20–21)
- Wavering or doubting healing (James 1:6–8, Mark 11:22–24)
- Eyes fixated on symptoms rather than on God (Heb. 11:1, 2 Cor. 4:18 & 5:7)
- Being hindered by the presence of unbelievers (Mark 6:1–6, Mark 5:35–42)
- Failure to ask God for healing (2 Chron. 16:12, 1 John 5:14–15, John 14:14, John 16:24)
- Not discerning the Lord's Body in Communion (1 Cor. 11:27–31)

Issues related to sin
- Unconfessed or cherished sin (Jer. 15:19a, 1 Pet 2:1)
- Lukewarmness (Rev. 3:15–16)
- Unforgiveness (Col. 3:13, Matt. 18:21–35, James 5:16)
- Bitterness (Heb. 12:14–16, James 3:14–15)
- Asking with wrong motives (James 4:2–3)
- Negative speaking (Matt. 12:37, Prov. 18:21, Rom. 10:9–10, Num. 14:27–2)
- Failure to examine our hearts (1 Cor. 11:29–31)

Issues related to perseverance
- Dictating to God the method or timing (2 Kings 5:1–14)
- Unwillingness to persevere (James 1:2–4, 1 Pet. 5:10, Heb. 12:1–3)
- Failure to persevere when faith is tested (Heb. 3:14, 10:35–39)
- Hardheartedness (John 12:40)

Issues related to wrong teaching, misinterpretation, or ignorance of Scripture

- Thinking God wants us sick or suffering (Matt. 14:14, Mark 1:40–41)
- Failure to understand the authority of supernatural law over natural law (2 Pet. 1:3–4, Eph. 1:18–20, 2 Cor. 5:7)
- Lack of understanding that sickness can be a spirit which needs to be cast out (Matt. 17:14–18, Luke 13:10–13)
- Not knowing how to receive our healing from Christ (Hosea 4:6)
- Preconceived ideas about how healing should or can take place (1 Kings 5:1–14, Isa. 43:18–19)
- Hearing a negative diagnosis and accepting it without seeking God (Num. 14:36–37, 2 Chron. 16:12, and Mark 5:26)

Chapter 9

Here are some Scriptures to help you understand the spiritual battle and your authority. All are from RSVCE.

"Behold, I have given you authority to tread upon serpents and scorpions, and over all the power of the enemy; and nothing shall hurt you." (Luke 10:19)

"You are my hammer and weapon of war: with you I break nations in pieces; with you I destroy kingdoms." (Jer. 51:20)

"Finally, be strong in the Lord and in the strength of his might. Put on the whole armor of God, that you may be able to stand against the wiles of the devil. For we are not contending against flesh and blood, but against the principalities, against the powers, against the world rulers of this present darkness, against the spiritual hosts of wickedness in the heavenly places. Therefore take the whole armor of God, that you may be able to withstand in the evil day, and having done all, to stand. Stand therefore, having girded your loins with truth, and having put on the breastplate of righteousness, and having shod your feet with the equipment of the gospel of peace; besides all these, taking the shield of faith, with which you can quench all the flaming darts of the evil one. And take the helmet of salvation, and the sword of the Spirit, which is the word of God." (Eph. 6:10–17)

"Submit yourselves therefore to God. Resist the devil and he will flee from you." (James 4:7)

"You are of God, and have overcome them; for he who is in you is greater than he who is in the world." (1 John:44)

"For though we live in the world we are not carrying on a worldly war, for the weapons of our warfare are not worldly but have divine power to destroy strongholds. We destroy arguments and every proud obstacle to the knowledge of God, and take every thought captive to obey Christ." (2 Cor. 10:3–5)

"Be sober, be watchful. Your adversary the devil prowls around like a roaring lion, seeking someone to devour. Resist him, firm in your faith." (1 Pet. 5:8–9)

"No weapon that is fashioned against you shall prosper, and you shall confute every tongue that rises against you in judgment. This is the heritage of the servants of the Lord and their vindication from me, says the Lord." (Isa. 54:17)

"In all these things, we are more than conquerors through Him who loved us." (Rom. 8:37)

"But thanks be to God, who gives us the victory through our Lord Jesus Christ." (1 Cor. 15:57)

"'Not by might nor by power, but by My Spirit,' says the Lord of hosts." (Zech. 4:6)

"But the Lord is faithful; he will strengthen you and guard you from evil." (2 Thess. 3:3)

"The thief comes only to steal and kill and destroy. I came that they may have life and have it abundantly." (John 10:10)

"Do not fear them, for the Lord your God is the one fighting for you." (Deut. 3:22)

"What then shall we say to this? If God is for us, who is against us?" (Rom. 8:31)

"Through thee we push down our foes; through thy name we tread down our assailants." (Ps. 44:5)

"Have I not commanded you? Be strong and of good courage; be not frightened, neither be dismayed; for the Lord your God is with you wherever you go." (Joshua 1:9)

"For thou didst gird me with strength for the battle; thou didst make my assailants sink under me." (Ps. 18:39)

"He who dwells in the shelter of the Most High, who abides in the shadow of the Almighty, will say to the Lord, 'My refuge and my fortress; my God, in whom I trust.' For he will deliver you from the snare of the fowler and from the deadly pestilence; he will cover you with his pinions, and under his wings you will find refuge; his faithfulness is a shield and buckler." (Ps. 91:1–4)

Chapter 11

I have included some Bible verses for meditating on God's love for us. Pray these Scripture, and make them personal. You are God's beloved and the one His heart seeks after!

O Lord, You have searched me and known me.
You know when I sit down and when I rise up;
You understand my thought from afar.
You scrutinize my path and my lying down,
And are intimately acquainted with all my ways.
Even before there is a word on my tongue,
Behold, O Lord, You know it all.
You have enclosed me behind and before,
And laid Your hand upon me.
Such knowledge is too wonderful for me;
It is too high, I cannot attain to it.
Where can I go from Your Spirit?
Or where can I flee from Your presence?
If I ascend to heaven, You are there;
If I make my bed in Sheol, behold, You are there.
If I take the wings of the dawn,
If I dwell in the remotest part of the sea,
Even there Your hand will lead me,
And Your right hand will lay hold of me.
If I say, "Surely the darkness will overwhelm me,
And the light around me will be night,"
Even the darkness is not dark to You,
And the night is as bright as the day.
Darkness and light are alike to You.
For You formed my inward parts;
You wove me in my mother's womb.
I will give thanks to You, for I am fearfully and wonderfully made;
Wonderful are Your works,
And my soul knows it very well.
My frame was not hidden from You,

When I was made in secret,
And skillfully wrought in the depths of the earth;
Your eyes have seen my unformed substance;
And in Your book were all written.
The days that were ordained for me,
When as yet there was not one of them.
How precious also are Your thoughts to me, O God!
How vast is the sum of them!
If I should count them, they would outnumber the sand.
When I awake, I am still with You. (Ps. 139:1–18).

"For I am his workmanship, created in Christ Jesus for good works, which God prepared beforehand, that I should walk in them." (Eph. 2:10)

"See what kind of love the Father has given to me, that I should be called a child of God; and so I am." (1 John 3:31)

"But I am a chosen race, a royal priesthood, a holy nation, a people for his own possession, that I may proclaim the excellencies of him who called me out of darkness into his marvelous light." (1 Pet. 2:9–10)

"So I have come to know and to believe the love that God has for me. God is love, and whoever abides in love abides in God, and God abides in him." (1 John 4:16)

"I praise you, for I am fearfully and wonderfully made." (Ps. 139:14)

"The Lord appeared . . . I have loved you with an everlasting love; therefore I have continued my faithfulness to you." (Jer. 31:3)

"Because you are precious in my eyes, and honored, and I love you." (Isa. 43:4)

References

Scriptures and verses taken from
- *Catechism of the Catholic Church.* 1994. Liguori, MO: Liguori Publications.
- *Holy Bible: English Standard Version.* 2001. Wheaton, IL: Crossway Bibles.
- *Holy Bible: New American Standard Edition.* 1995. La Habra, CA: Lockman Foundation.
- *Holy Bible: Revised Standard Version Catholic Edition.* Copyrighted 1946, 1952, 1957, 1965, 1966, 2006. Washington, D.C.: Division of Christian Education of the National Council of the Churches of Christ in the USA.

Chapter 1
1. Marni Feuerman, "21 Warning Signs of an Emotionally Abusive Relationship," *PsychCentral*, (July 2018), https://psychcentral.com/blog/21-warning-signs-of-an-emotionally-abusive-relationship/.

Chapter 2
1. Congregation for the Doctrine of the Faith, "Instruction on Prayers for Healing," *L'Osservatore Romano,* (December 2000), 9.
2. C. Bernard Ruffin, *Padre Pio: The True Story,* (Huntington, Our Sunday Visitor, 1991), 260.

Chapter 4
1. Joyce Meyer, *Battlefield of the Mind,* (Hatchette, Warner Faith Book Publishers, 1997).

Chapter 5
1. Herbert Benson, John W. Lehmann, Mark D. Epstein, Ralph F. Goldman, "Science Watch; Heat from Meditation," *New York Times,* (New York, NY), Feb 9, 1982.
2. Aurin Squire, *The Holocaust and Jack Schwarz, Six*

Perfections, (December 28, 2012), http://sixperfections.blogspot.com/2012/12/the-holocaust-and-jack-schwarz.html.

3. Sheldon Sheps, M.D., *Anxiety: A Cause of High Blood Pressure,* (Rochester, MN: Mayo Clinic, January 2019).
4. John Sarno, MD, *Mindbody Prescription,* (New York: Little Brown and Co, 2007), 144.
5. Joyce Meyer, *Battlefield of the Mind,* (Hatchette, Warner Faith Book Publishers, 1997), 13.
6. Lorie Johnson, *The Deadly Consequences of Unforgiveness,* CBN News (June 22, 2015), https://www1.cbn.com/cbnnews/healthscience/2015/June/The-Deadly-Consequences-of-Unforgiveness.
7. *Forgiveness: Your Health Depends on it,* https://www.hopkinsmedicine.org/health/wellness-and-prevention/forgiveness-your-health-depends-on-it.

Chapter 6
1. C.S. Lewis, *The Problem of Pain,* (London, UK, Harper Collins edition, 1977).

Chapter 7
1. Doctrinal Commission of the International Catholic Charismatic Renewal Services (ICCRS), *Guidelines of Prayer for Healing,* (Vatican, Vera Cruz Communications, 2012).
2. Tony Melendez Biography, *Tony Melendez Official Website,* https://www.tonymelendez.com/.
3. Christian History, "Fanny Crosby; Prolific and Blind Christian Writer," *Christianity Today* (2000) https://www.christianitytoday.com/history/people/poets/fanny-crosby.html.
4. Grace Pike, "Strength Amidst Suffering: Lessons from the Life of Charlotte Elliott," *The Spurgeon Center for Biblical Preaching,* (2019), https://www.spurgeon.org/resource-library/blog-entries/strength-amidst-suffering-lessons-from-the-life-of-charlotte-elliott.

5. Sean Coughlan, "Parents who Saved their Only Child by Giving her Away*, BBC News*, (August 3, 2018), https://www.bbc.com/news/education-44932052

6. Allie Firestone, "Father's Day Heroes," *Gimundo*, (June 17, 2011), www.gimundo.com

Chapter 8

1. Merlin Carothers, *Prison to Praise*, (Carothers, 1970).

Chapter 9

1. Gillis Triplett, "Spiritual Warfare 101," *Gillis Triplett Ministries*, (March 17, 2020) https://www.gillistriplett.com/healing/articles/tactics.html.

2. Zenit staff, "John Paul II Explains the New Age of Christ," *Vatican Dicasteries*, (Feb 14, 2001) https://zenit.org/articles/john-paul-ii-explains-the-new-age-of-christ/

3. *St Anthony's Brief*, (2019), rosarybay.com.

4. The Catholic Warrior, "Spiritual Warfare Prayers," (Valentine Publishing House, 2017), https://www.catholicwarriors.com/pages/warfare_prayers.htm

Chapter 11

1. Bob Marley, *The Future Is The Beginning: The Words and Wisdom of Bob Marley,* (New York, NY, Crown Archetype, 2012).

2. Thomas Aquinas, translated by Fathers of the English Dominican Province, *Summa Theologiae, q73,* (New York, NY, Benziger Brothers, 1947).

3. Fr. Pedro Arrupe, SJ, *Falling in Love, Finding all things in God,* Loyola Press, (2009), www.ignatianspirituality.com

About the Author

Tammy Stanek, RN, has continued education in the areas of nutrition and natural health. She also has certification in Theological and Pastoral Studies from Christ the King Seminary in East Aurora, New York.

Tammy is widowed and the mother of three adult children who support her two passions: her deep faith and her love of helping people. She is very active in her parish via music ministry, healing and prayer ministries, and catechesis; she has consecrated her life to God as a consecrated widow.

After many years of suffering and loss, her faith walk became instrumental in healing. Now she hopes to help others in their journey. She is warmly open to sharing her faith, as well as her knowledge and experience.

Made in the USA
Middletown, DE
03 June 2021